I0762502

*To every young adventurer
seeking the magic of the great outdoors.*

The Nature of Our National Parks

By Alexander M. Rigby

Illustrated by Qu Lan

Publisher & Creative Director
Ilona Oppenheim

Art & Design Director
Jefferson Quintana

Editorial Director
Lisa McGuinness

Publishing Director
Jessica Faroy

Copyeditor
Robin Miller

This product is made of FSC®-certified and other controlled material.

Tra Publishing is committed to sustainability in its materials and practices.

Printed and bound in China by Artron Art Co., Ltd.

The Nature of Our National Parks was first published in the United States by Tra Publishing in 2026.

ISBN: 978-1-9620983-5-9

Tra Publishing
245 NE 37th Street
Miami, FL 33137
trapublishing.com

1 2 3 4 5 6 7 8 9 10

THE NATURE OF OUR NATIONAL PARKS

ALEXANDER M. RIGBY
ILLUSTRATED BY QU LAN

tra.publishing

M E X I C O

CANADA
58
59
1
60
63
2
3
61
62
4
5
10
9
6
7
8

The wonders of nature called out to me. So, when I was young, I decided to explore our country's amazing landscapes. Visiting every national park in America was at the top of my list.

I packed up an old camper van and left my home in Western Pennsylvania to start an epic road trip across the nation. I was excited to visit our wild, magical lands, from sea to shining sea.

ACADIA

MAINE • ESTABLISHED 1919 • 77 SQUARE MILES

The stone coast of Maine was where I stopped first. I arrived at Mount Desert Island after a long drive and walked along the high sea cliffs near Otter Point, watching in awe as waves crashed against the rocks.

Wanting to get even higher and see more of the coast and the island's mountainous edges, I hiked the Beehive Trail next, climbing a steep path to get to the top. When I reached one of the trail's highest points, the Atlantic Ocean stretched out toward the horizon, with no end in sight. I noticed other small islands that dotted the waterways beyond Bar Harbor that looked like giant whales breaching the surface.

A red fox came out of the trees and sat on a rock not far from where I stood. "Can you believe these views?" I asked it, even though I knew it couldn't answer me. The fox stared at me and yipped before disappearing as quickly as it had arrived.

Back down at the camper, I drove around to visit the other parts of the park, where more mountains, lakes, and forests waited. The famous Bass Harbor Head lighthouse along the water was a worthy site to visit, too. In addition to the main island, you can explore even more gorgeous rocky coastlines on the Schoodic Peninsula and Isle au Haut.

While I was in Acadia, I detailed the flora, fauna, and formations I noticed and learned about in a journal I'd brought along. I decided I'd write about the nature I discovered at every park during my adventure.

❶ **RED SPRUCE**
Picea rubens
Well adapted to cold climates, this tree can withstand Maine's chilly temperatures.

❷ **EASTERN WHITE PINE**
Pinus strobus
One of the most common pine trees in Acadia, this species reaches some of the tallest heights of any tree found in eastern North America.

❸ **ATLANTIC PUFFIN**
Fratercula arctica
To see these adorable birds, you'll need to take a tour boat from Acadia to Petit Manan Island, which is a smaller and more remote isle east of the park.

❹ **RED FOX** *Vulpes vulpes*
If you're lucky, you may spot a flash of red fur among all the blue and green, as this omnivorous mammal searches for other animals and plants to eat across the park.

❺ **CADILLAC MOUNTAIN**
The highest mountain (1,530 feet) on the Atlantic Ocean shoreline in the United States, it's often the first place in the nation to see the sunrise.

KID-FRIENDLY HIKE
Jordan Pond Path
A mostly flat 3.3-mile loop trail that encircles the pond and offers scenic views of the nearby mountains, including the Bubbles.

SHENANDOAH

VIRGINIA • ESTABLISHED 1935 • 308 SQUARE MILES

After Acadia, I climbed back into my camper and drove south. The Appalachian Mountains of Virginia were my next stop.

Once I arrived, I hiked Old Rag, scrambling past massive boulders to reach the top. It wasn't easy, but it was worth it. There were layers and layers of blue ridge peaks, the setting sun lighting them up.

More views of these ancient mountains came into view the next day as I hiked along the short Stony Man Summit Trail, where sharp gray rocks and bright-green trees created shadows against each other.

I took the famous Skyline Drive out of the park, saving the prettiest views that are easily seen from the road for last.

❶ MOREL MUSHROOM

Morchella esculenta

One of many fungi found in the park that breaks down and recycles organic matter, this species is a popular edible variety. But be careful, many mushrooms are poisonous to eat!

❷ WHITE-TAILED DEER

Odocoileus virginianus

A common mammal found across the United States that is most active at dusk and dawn. Males grow antlers, which they shed each year.

❸ DARK HOLLOW FALLS

Take a short hike downhill right off of Skyline Drive to reach this 70-foot cascade, which rushes down dark rock walls in multiple ribbons of white.

❶

❸

❷

NEW RIVER GORGE

WEST VIRGINIA • ESTABLISHED 2020 • 114 SQUARE MILES

I headed three hours west to get to the gorge and the river that runs through it. As I arrived, I drove over the large steel bridge that spans the river gorge. It was an impressive introduction to this natural feature, which cuts through these West Virginian mountains.

At the visitor center, I chatted with a park ranger who taught me that the New River is actually one of the oldest rivers in the world. After he handed me a park map, he persuaded me to join his rafting tour. We bumped up and down the rapids, getting splashed with white, foamy water. Traveling on the New River, we cut through the Appalachians, learning of their folklore.

❶ GREAT RHODODENDRON

Rhododendron maximum

The state flower of West Virginia, this large plant is known for blooming in shades of light, whitish-pink.

❷ BALD EAGLE

Haliaeetus leucocephalus

Having recently returned to live in the park after years away, the bald eagle is a powerful bird of prey that lives in areas near water with tall trees, so its fishing and nesting needs are met. It is an American icon that's found in every state except for Hawaii.

❸ GRANDVIEW

Stop at this spot 1,400 feet above where the river carves a curved path through the mountains for outstanding views of the gorge.

GREAT SMOKY MOUNTAINS

NORTH CAROLINA & TENNESSEE • ESTABLISHED 1934 • 816 SQUARE MILES

I drove into the heart of the Appalachians to explore the Smokies. As I entered the park in the morning, a mama black bear and her cubs crossed by right in front of me! At the visitor center, I told a park ranger about it. "You've always got to be bear aware when you're here!" she said. I took the warning to heart before I continued on.

A light layer of fog covered the mountains in a fascinating blue-tinged haze, giving them the "smoky" appearance they're named for.

I climbed to the top of a mountain called Kuwohi (also known as Clingmans Dome), where a human-made tower straddles the state line. The bright sun burned off the fog as I climbed, allowing me to see some of the highest peaks in the East from the tower's upper platform. This part of the park was crowded, and I missed feeling like the wilderness was just mine.

❸

With 848 miles of trails, ancient mountains that are home to all kinds of species, stunning vistas along the park's roads, and many accessible waterfalls, it's no wonder this is our country's most visited park!

Still, I yearned to be alone in nature like I had been at some of my previous parks. So the next day, after camping overnight, I hiked through the woods to see the Chimney Tops, which are harder to get to and usually have fewer visitors. Hiking through the lush green forest and passing by many streams and waterfalls before climbing high into the mountains made my heart happy.

❶ FLAME AZALEA
Rhododendron calendulaceum
Blooming at various elevations across the park, this shrub has flowers that come in shades of yellow, orange, and red.
❷ YELLOW BIRCH
Betula alleghaniensis
This tree, which can be found across the park, gets its name from the golden-hued color of its often-peeling bark.
❸ BLACK BEAR
Ursus americanus
There are nearly 2,000 bears to be found here, which is part of the reason they're considered the park's most famous residents. Cubs stay with their mothers for up to 18 months.
❹ HOODED WARBLER
Setophaga citrina
This black-and-yellow bird can be found across the park's forests, often in the understory beneath the tallest trees.
❺ CHIMNEY TOPS
One of the few bare rock summits in the Smokies, this 4,724-foot peak has two pointy knobs that can be seen from the Chimney Tops Trail.
KID-FRIENDLY HIKE
Laurel Falls Trail
A mostly paved 2.6-mile round-trip hike through the forest to an 80-foot waterfall.
4
5
2
1

1

CONGAREE

SOUTH CAROLINA • ESTABLISHED 2003 • 42 SQUARE MILES

Walking along the boardwalk through the Southern swamp-like lands of Congaree, I learned it was possible for trees to have knees. My park map explained these "knees" of the bald cypress trees are actually exposed roots that help them remain stable when flood waters surge in.

Even though it's regularly called a swamp, Congaree is better described as a floodplain, which often fills with murky water, submerging the old-growth forest. I visited many of the park's lakes and creeks, strolling along the elevated boardwalks and trails, fully exploring this inspiring, old, wet woodland.

The park is home to some of the tallest trees east of the Mississippi River, which isn't hard to believe, as I had to crane my neck backward to see some of the treetops!

❷

❸

❶ BALD CYPRESS
Taxodium distichum
Some of the bald cypress trees in Congaree are over 500 years old. The park protects the largest remaining old-growth bottomland hardwood forest in the United States.

❷ EASTERN BOX TURTLE
Terrapene carolina carolina
This turtle has a high, domelike shell to protect it, which is usually brownish-black and covered with a yellow or orange radiating pattern of spots and lines.

❸ CEDAR CREEK
Offering a 15-mile marked trail for kayakers to follow, this blackwater creek winds through the heart of the park.

BISCAYNE

FLORIDA • ESTABLISHED 1980 • 270 SQUARE MILES

After Congaree, my camper carried me south. I returned to the coast for the first time since Acadia, arriving at Biscayne Bay. Much more tropical than coastal Maine, Biscayne is home to mangrove shorelines, over 30 small islands, and impressive coral reefs, which are part of a 150-mile-long chain that extends to the lower Florida Keys.

Because 95 percent of this park is ocean, it's a great place to snorkel or scuba-dive if you want to spot the wide array of sea life that lives here.

Instead of trying any underwater activities, I took a boat tour out to Boca Chita Key, one of the small islands far off the mainland. Out on the water, I could see the huge size of the bay, as the ocean stretched for miles between the island and the distant Miami skyline.

❶ RED MANGROVE
Rhizophora mangle
This salt-tolerant tree grows in the ocean, with its aerial prop roots arching above sea level. The shore of Biscayne Bay is covered by an extensive mangrove forest, which helps prevent erosion.

❷ FLORIDA MANATEE
Trichechus manatus latirostris
A large aquatic mammal native to warm coastal waters, this species feeds on underwater plants and uses its highly sensitive whiskers to navigate.

❸ BOCA CHITA KEY
Just above the northernmost Florida Keys, this island boasts a picturesque 65-foot lighthouse made of native coral rock. Feel free to climb its stairs to the top!

2

EVERGLADES

FLORIDA • ESTABLISHED 1947 • 2,358 SQUARE MILES

Once back on the mainland, I headed west to the Everglades, a huge area of wetlands that make up the largest tropical wilderness in the United States! This vast ecosystem is often called the "River of Grass," because of the shallow, slow-moving river system that's covered by sawgrass marshes.

The many different habitats you can see in this park include cypress swamps, wet prairies, and mangrove forests. The Everglades are home to alligators, crocodiles, and even Florida panthers. I took a stroll along the Anhinga Trail and spotted some cool tropical birds poking their long necks through the tall grass. An alligator floated to the water's surface to soak up some of the sun's rays.

A friendly old man with thick circular glasses watching the alligator beside me offered a suggestion: "If you want to see what this park's really like, take a kayak out on the Nine Mile Pond canoe trail."

I did as he suggested. Paddling through the connected shallow marshes later that afternoon, I was lucky enough to see many great egrets and more alligators pass.

❶ SAWGRASS
Cladium jamaicense
This plant can be found in sawgrass marshes across the park, thriving in areas that are wet year-round.

❷ FLORIDA BUTTERFLY ORCHID *Encyclia tampensis*
An orchid that grows on trees, this plant pulls moisture and nutrients from the air, rain, and surrounding organic debris without harming the plant it lives on.

❸ GREAT EGRET
Casmerodius albus
A large, bright-white wading bird that stands over four feet tall, it feeds across a variety of wetlands.

❹ AMERICAN ALLIGATOR
Alligator mississippiensis
Known for having an incredibly strong bite, the American Alligator's mouth is full of 74 to 80 teeth, which help it consume all kinds of prey.

❺ WEST LAKE
You can visit this lake by taking an easy half mile stroll on the boardwalk trail that wanders through a forest of mangroves, or by paddling along the West Lake Canoe Trail.

KID-FRIENDLY HIKE
Gumbo Limbo Trail
A paved 0.4-mile round-trip trail that weaves through a shaded jungle of gumbo limbo trees and other plants.

2

DRY TORTUGAS

FLORIDA • ESTABLISHED 1992 • 100 SQUARE MILES

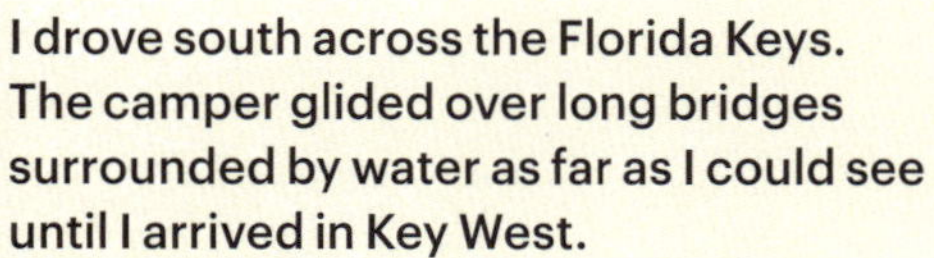

I drove south across the Florida Keys. The camper glided over long bridges surrounded by water as far as I could see until I arrived in Key West.

A two-hour boat ride from Key West across 68 miles of open ocean dropped me off at Garden Key. Because this park is accessible only by boat or seaplane, it's often overlooked, but I was glad to have made the journey.

I learned about the history of Fort Jefferson—a huge fort on the island—as I walked along its tall walls. The fort has great views of the surrounding ocean, where coral reefs, tropical fish, and sea turtles thrive in shallow depths. After circling the fort, I got to snorkel in the crystal-clear turquoise waters, spotting many colorful fish as I swam!

❶

❶ SEA OATS
Uniola paniculata
This plant helps protect the beaches it grows on, as its tall leaves trap wind-blown sand to promote dune growth, while its deep roots help to stabilize them.

❷ MAGNIFICENT FRIGATEBIRD
Fregata magnificens
Known for its 7- to 8-foot wingspan and the striking bright-red throat sac males have, this bird can be seen diving toward the sea to snatch fish that swim near its surface.

❸ GARDEN KEY
The second largest island in the park, this key is home to Fort Jefferson, a massive brick structure soldiers built here in the mid-1800s.

VIRGIN ISLANDS

US VIRGIN ISLANDS • ESTABLISHED 1956 • 23 SQUARE MILES

To get to my next park, I had to take to the skies, flying from Miami to St. Thomas. The US claimed this group of tropical isles in the Caribbean Sea as a territory in 1917.

After ferrying over to St. John, I visited the northern beaches, swimming in the refreshing waters of Trunk Bay.

Nearly two-thirds of this island is part of the national park, so there's a lot to explore, like tropical forests, steep mountains with epic views, and white-sand beaches that lead to crystal blue-green waters filled with brightly colored fish and other sea creatures.

My favorite part of the visit was hiking the Ram Head Trail where, from the tops of steep cliffs, I saw stunning views of the many nearby islands while the ocean swirled below.

❶ TURK'S CAP CACTUS

Melocactus intortus

A barrel-shaped cactus that often grows along cliff formations, it's easily recognized by the red tubular structure protruding from its top.

❷ SPOTTED EAGLE RAY

Aetobatus narinari

This dark-colored ray is covered with white spots and rings, which makes seeing them a visual treat. Don't swim too close though—they have poisonous barbed stingers!

❸ TRUNK BAY

Stop and see this amazing spot from the overlook along the park's road, then drive down to the shore for a swim. It's known as one of the best beaches in the world for a reason!

HOT SPRINGS

ARKANSAS • ESTABLISHED 1921 • 9 SQUARE MILES

Another flight took me back to Miami, where I picked up the camper and hit the road again, heading out West. Before long, I arrived in Hot Springs, one of our smallest parks, which happens to be located in the middle of a town. I found it a bit surprising that this mostly human-made place is a national park since it's so different from the other nature-based parks—but I wanted to see it anyway.

I visited the many historic mansion-like buildings lined up on Bathhouse Row, each one with its own style. These buildings used to house fancy baths and spas where people could relax and rest in the warm waters of the hot springs that burst forth from the ground.

The hot springs are heated by the earth's warm inner layers before they are pushed through cracks in the sandstone along the western slope of Hot Springs Mountain.

After exploring the bathhouses, I hiked the mountain trail, where views of the quaint town tucked into the mountain valley could be seen from above.

❶ DWARF SPIDERWORT

Tradescantia longipes
This plant has bright purple flowers that bloom close to the ground.

❷ BEE BALM

Monarda fistulosa
During spring, this fragrant wildflower attracts bees to its pink and purple blossoms to collect nectar. It can be spotted growing along the park's forested hills and valleys.

❸ GROUNDHOG

Marmota monax
Also known as a woodchuck, this mammal uses its sharp claws to dig burrows.

❹ AMERICAN BULLFROG

Lithobates catesbeianus
An amphibian that lives most of its life in or near water, this frog gets its name from the bull-like sound males make during breeding season.

❺ HOT WATER CASCADE

Head over to Arlington Lawn to see this hot spring—the largest one visible in the park—which flows out of a hillside and falls into two pools below.

KID-FRIENDLY HIKE

Grand Promenade
Running parallel behind Bathhouse Row, this brick-lined pathway is about a half-mile long. It's a pleasant place to go for a stroll.

BIG BEND

TEXAS • ESTABLISHED 1944 • 1,252 SQUARE MILES

Getting to Big Bend took a good bit of time, because it's in the middle of nowhere and not on the way to anything else. As the popular saying goes, "you don't get here by accident!"

This huge park in remote West Texas is tucked along a big bend in the Rio Grande (hence the name!), which is the river that forms a large portion of our border with Mexico. The park protects a massive area where the Chihuahuan Desert and the Chisos Mountains collide, preserving the ecosystem that thrives here from any negative human-made influences.

I was amazed by the terrain when I finally arrived, as the mountainous desert landscape felt so distinct compared to what I'd seen previously in the eastern parks.

While hiking the Lost Mine Trail into the mountains, I thought about all the time I'd spent exploring the parks so far and was excited to have lots more to go.

I ended my time at this park by hiking through a boulder-filled desert landscape, scrambling up a hill to see Balanced Rock. As I took in the unique sights nature had made, a Texas horned lizard crawled onto a rock near me and another hiker. "I love the way the rocks balance against one another and create a window to see the mountains through," she said, not even noticing the lizard. I laughed and replied, "I really love it, too."

❶ HAVARD AGAVE
Agave havardiana
The largest agave in the park, whose leaves have a blue-gray color, typically only bloom once in their lives after growing for 20 to 50 years.

❷ OCOTILLO
Fouquieria splendens
Also called the vine cactus, this plant's tall gray stalks only produce leaves after strong rains.

❸ TEXAS HORNED LIZARD
Phrynosoma cornutum
A spiky-bodied reptile that loves to lounge in the sun, this species is known for eating up to 100 ants a day. It is the largest-bodied and most widely distributed horned lizard in the western United States.

❹ JAVELINA
Dicotyles tajacu
While this species is often mistaken for a pig, it's actually part of a different family. They can be found eating plants and fruits across the park.

❺ SANTA ELENA CANYON
It's possible to hike into this impressive canyon and walk along the steep rock walls, which border the Rio Grande on both sides.

KID-FRIENDLY HIKE
Window View Trail
This short, paved 0.3-mile loop trail offers great views of the surrounding Chisos Basin.

2

GUADALUPE MOUNTAINS

TEXAS • ESTABLISHED 1972 • 135 SQUARE MILES

About four hours north of Big Bend, the highest mountains in Texas rise toward the sky. This is a landscape where mountains, forests, and deserts come together, creating a unique ecosystem to explore.

The Guadalupe Mountains shoot up more than 3,000 feet higher than the Chihuahuan Desert that surrounds them, creating an impressive sight. El Capitan, a 1,000-foot-tall limestone cliff, is the park's most dramatic formation, as it steals your attention with its sheer height.

At the visitor center, I discovered that the park holds the world's largest Permian fossil reef, which includes fossils of marine plants and animals that lived in an ancient sea here millions of years ago.

After learning all I could, I took a walk through McKittrick Canyon, visited the gypsum sand dunes, and admired the sun setting behind the peaks as the evening arrived.

❶ PRICKLY PEAR
Opuntia spinosibacca
A type of cactus that can be found throughout the Southwest region, this variety is known for its yellow flowers and red juicy fruits.

❷ BLACK-TAILED JACKRABBIT
Lepus californicus
Also known as the American desert hare, this jackrabbit uses its large ears to radiate heat away from its body to keep cool. It doesn't migrate or hibernate during winter, remaining in the same territory year-round.

❸ GUADALUPE PEAK
The highest peak in Texas, which rises 8,751 feet. You can hike to the summit for remarkable views of the park by following the 4.2-mile trail (each way).

CARLSBAD CAVERNS

NEW MEXICO • ESTABLISHED 1930 • 73 SQUARE MILES

Just across the Texas–New Mexico border, a dreamlike cave exists underground. Millions of years ago, this limestone cavern started to form, creating rooms large enough to walk through, where both stalactites and stalagmites abound.

Stalactites grow from minerals dripping down from the ceiling like icicles with pointed tips, while stalagmites rise up from the cavern's floors in more rounded, mound shapes.

I walked through the cave on a guided tour from the natural entrance, where thousands of bats were hanging from the cave's roof, tucked up in the dark. We couldn't see them, but we could smell them!

The tour took us all the way to the Big Room, where tons of alien-looking formations deep in the earth can be found. A few of my favorite spots were Fairyland, Witch's Finger, Rock of Ages, and Devil's Spring.

❶ BUTTERFLY WEED
Asclepias tuberosa
Known for blooming in the park (aboveground) every year, this milkweed plant is an important nectar source for butterflies, which are attracted to its bright warm color.

❷ MEXICAN FREE-TAILED BAT
Tadarida brasiliensis
This flying mammal weighs only about a half ounce and has an 11- to 14-inch wingspan. A large colony wows visitors with their evening flights out of the natural cave entrance and into the sky.

❸ BIG ROOM
At almost 4,000 feet long, 625 feet wide, and 255 feet tall, this enormous room full of fascinating formations is the largest underground chamber in North America.

WHITE SANDS

NEW MEXICO • ESTABLISHED 2019 • 228 SQUARE MILES

I drove the camper three hours west to see the largest white sand dunes in the world. The dunes cover 275 square miles and the sand is made of white gypsum crystals, which gather in the Tularosa Basin in the shadow of the San Andres Mountains.

Hiking across these white sands, I noticed all kinds of patterns and textures created by the wind on the surface of the dunes, some of which reach up to 60 feet high! While there are markers in the sand that show where the trails go to help prevent visitors from getting lost, people can pretty much wander wherever they like across the powdery dunes, which create ridgelines against the sky.

As I knelt down to get a closer look at a cool pattern of lines, a tarantula crawled up beside me. The way its many legs moved across the sand made me realize it was studying the texture of the grains with its touch. “Goes to show you, sometimes the magic’s in the little things,” I said aloud, in awe of the spider. Normally I’d be afraid of a tarantula, but the wonder of this park had helped me feel fearless, so I didn’t mind its company.

❶ SOAPTREE YUCCA
Yucca elata
Popping up across the dune field, this yucca has a whorl of leaves with a long slender stem growing up from its center, where cream-colored flowers bloom in spring.

❷ DESERT SPOON
Dasylirion wheeleri
This plant gets its name from the spoon-like depression at its leafy base.

❸ DESERT BLONDE TARANTULA
Aphonopelma chalcodes
These large, hairy spiders have terrible eyesight, which requires them to use their sense of touch to navigate the world. They make their homes in burrows and crevices, of which there are many in White Sands.

❹ KIT FOX
Vulpes macrotis
The smallest wild canine found in America, this tiny fox is the size of an adult chihuahua

❺ ALKALI FLAT
A large, flat area of selenite crystals in a dried-out, ancient lakebed, this feature stretches on for miles between the mountains and the dunes. You can't walk onto it, but you can see it from the end of the Alkali Flat Trail.

KID-FRIENDLY HIKE
Dune Life Nature Trail
A 1-mile loop trail at the edge of the dune field, where desert vegetation and gypsum sand dunes intersect.

3

SAGUARO

ARIZONA • ESTABLISHED 1994 • 143 SQUARE MILES

Split into two sections on either side of the city of Tucson, this park is full of the iconic saguaro cacti. The Sonoran Desert landscape dominates here. I was able to get up-close views of the gigantic cacti while trekking up the Signal Hill Trail. The hot, sunny weather made me work up a sweat.

As the day faded toward night, I decided to head to Gates Pass. This fantastic spot right outside the park was the perfect location to watch an incredible sunset in the desert valley, where I spotted tons of saguaros creating dark shadows against a glowing, orange-and-red sky.

❶ SAGUARO CACTUS

Carnegiea gigantea

Able to grow up to 40 feet tall and live for more than 150 years, this icon of Arizona is a keystone species, which provides food and habitat for many creatures in the park.

❷ GILA WOODPECKER

Melanerpes uropygialis

A medium-sized woodpecker with a black and white zebra-like pattern, it makes its nest in cavities in the sides of saguaros. Adult males can be recognized by the red caps on their heads.

❸ TANQUE VERDE RIDGE

This mountainous ridge in the eastern Rincon Mountain District of the park is formed by 1.4 billion-year-old granite rock. Hike the Tanque Verde Ridge Trail to see it!

PETRIFIED FOREST

ARIZONA • ESTABLISHED 1962 • 346 SQUARE MILES

This park in northeast Arizona is less of a forest and more of a graveyard for fallen, petrified trees that have transformed into crystal-like stone over thousands of years. Plus, there are tons of fossils that are millions of years old!

The landscape here has been shaped by wind and erosion, something I noticed while walking across the desert steppe and through the colorful badlands.

Parts of the park feel like another planet; the multicolored hills and ancient, crystalized tree trunks are an amazing sight to behold. Make sure you look at the petrified logs up close, as the colorful crystalline details forged within them over the eons are astonishing.

❶

❸

❶ ONE-SEED JUNIPER
Juniperus monosperma
One of the few live trees found in the park, this juniper grows on mesa tops where it must adapt to survive, its twisting branches a sign of its struggle to conserve scarce water.

❷ COLLARED LIZARD
Crotaphytus collaris
Named for the bands of black around its neck and shoulders, this lizard is able to run quickly on its two hind legs whenever it is in danger. Males look like colorful tiny dinosaurs, in shades of blue, green, and yellow.

❸ BLUE MESA
Walk along the Blue Mesa Trail to surround yourself with badlands of blue-and-purple clay, where petrified wood can also be found. Stop at one of the overlooks to view this mesmerizing place from above, too!

2

GRAND CANYON

ARIZONA • ESTABLISHED 1919 • 1,904 SQUARE MILES

When the Grand Canyon came into view for the first time, it felt like I was dreaming! Standing on the edge of the south rim, I peered across the miles-wide gorge, where warm-colored rocks drop down at steep angles toward where the Colorado River streams.

It's considered the most famous canyon in the world due to its immense size, the geological history you can see on the many different rock layers, and the diverse plant and animal species who live here.

I hiked into the canyon, walking along the Bright Angel Trail, passing by the canyon's walls, buttes, peaks, and ravines, which have all been carved by erosion and weathering across eons of time. The hike was easy because it was all downhill, but I knew to conserve my energy, as the way back up would be steep and a lot harder!

I realized that my life was just a small part of Earth's history, especially when compared with this millions-of-years-old canyon. I paused and said, "I want to see as much of the world as I can during my life," speaking this wish into existence.

A few small rocks fell off the ledge above me, so my gaze shifted upward, where I locked eyes with a large cougar perched on the orange cliff. Its sudden appearance caused my heart to race, but I got the sense it just wanted to watch me and all the other hikers pass by.

"You're already here," an older woman with a long white braid said to me then as she quickly trekked past me, her two hiking poles click-clacking on the ground as she moved. She must have heard what I'd just said. "To live a rich life, always lean into adventure and be willing to face the unknown," she said before waving goodbye and continuing down into the canyon.

❶ ARIZONA FISHHOOK CACTUS

Cochemiea grahamii

This small cactus prefers rocky or sandy soils and can be found at various elevations around the park. In spring, pink and purple flowers burst from its top.

❷ PINYON PINE

Pinus edulis

This evergreen is found in pinyon-juniper woodlands along the rim of the canyon. Its small cones produce large seeds called pine nuts.

❸ PINYON JAY

Gymnorhinus cyanocephalus

Known for its blue coloring, this bird has the perfect bill to retrieve pine nuts from the cones of pinyon trees.

❹ COUGAR *Puma concolor*

The largest carnivorous animal in the park, cougars are solitary animals with powerful bodies that allow them to leap and sprint short distances.

❺ COLORADO RIVER

The fifth longest river in the United States, it has carved the canyon over millions of years, cutting into the earth and eroding rock. While not easily visible from the rim, you can hike down to see where it flows at the canyon's bottom.

KID-FRIENDLY HIKE

Rim Trail

You'll be rewarded with fabulous views into the canyon from any part of this 13-mile long, mostly paved trail.

DEATH VALLEY

CALIFORNIA (AND NEVADA) • ESTABLISHED 1994 • 5,347 SQUARE MILES

I left Arizona and drove into California to visit the largest national park in the lower 48 states. Death Valley is a land of extremes, as it's the hottest, driest, and lowest park in the country. These harsh conditions made me think there wouldn't be much wildlife here, but as I explored the mountains, canyons, sand dunes, salt flats, and spring-fed oases across this enormous park, I learned of many species who call Death Valley home.

The vista at Dante's View was an epic way to see the vast size of the valley and how quickly the elevation changes across formations.

As night approached, I climbed the high piles of the Mesquite Flat Sand Dunes to watch the light fade on the sand and mountains in the distance as the sun set.

❶ DESERT GOLD

Geraea canescens

This slender daisy-like flower has yellow petals and grows a few feet tall. It's resistant to drought, and participates in super blooms when there's sufficient rainfall.

❷ DEATH VALLEY PUPFISH

Cyprinodon salinus

An endangered species found only in the park—at two locations, Salt Creek and Cottonball Marsh—this small fish can survive in water that's four times saltier than the ocean.

❸ BADWATER BASIN

At 282 feet below sea level, this expansive salt flat is the lowest point in North America. It covers nearly 200 square miles tucked beneath towering mountains. You can venture out to experience this unique landscape yourself.

1

JOSHUA TREE

CALIFORNIA • ESTABLISHED 1994 • 1,242 SQUARE MILES

I headed south and passed through the Mojave Desert until I reached the land of Joshua trees. These yucca plants (called Joshua trees) can be found all over the park, sometimes grouped together and other times spread out across wide-open spaces. Large boulders and rock formations abound here, and people come to climb them.

This is a land where deserts collide, as the higher and cooler Mojave meets the lower and hotter Colorado. The park's elevation spans from 536 feet to nearly 6,000 feet, and it boasts dry lakes, sand dunes, flat valleys, rugged mountains, and granite monoliths—quite the variety, if you ask me!

A walk along the Hall of Horrors trail granted me views of Joshua trees next to enormous rocks. Don't be fooled by the trail's name though, as the park's beauty far outshines anything scary to see.

❶ JOSHUA TREE

Yucca brevifolia

Confusingly, this species is not a tree, but a yucca that is confined mostly to the Mojave Desert. Its stout trunk leads to wobbly-looking arms with sharp, spiny-tipped, grayish-green leaves.

❷ COYOTE

Canis latrans

Smaller than its close relative, the gray wolf, this canine species can adapt to a variety of habitats. The ancient Navajo labeled it a trickster, and you may hear it howling if you're in the park at night.

❸ SKULL ROCK

This enormous granite rock has been eroded by rain water, creating two holes that resemble eye sockets, giving it a skull-like appearance.

HAWAII VOLCANOES

HAWAII • ESTABLISHED 1916 • 522 SQUARE MILES

To reach my twentieth park, I had to drive to Los Angeles, leave the camper at the airport, and fly to the island chain of Hawaii far out in the Pacific Ocean. Once I arrived, I made my way to the Big Island, where a park with two active volcanoes awaited me.

I peered into Kilauea's hot and steamy crater from its overlook, hoping it wouldn't erupt while I was so close, then traveled along the Chain of Craters Road until I reached the stunning Hōlei Sea Arch.

As I stood along the coast and studied the black rocky cliffs, which I'd learned had been formed by ancient lava flows, a strange-looking goose landed on the ground beside me and a teenaged boy with black hair who was sitting nearby. "I grew up on this island, and I still never get tired of visiting this place. Isn't it wild to be here, where lava spouts out of volcanoes and empties right into the sea?" he asked me.

I thought for a moment before I responded. "This place is magical. I wonder how many other spots on Earth are home to water and fire mixing like this." The bird made a soft cooing noise and scuttled away, the teenager departing shortly thereafter without saying anything else, leaving me alone on the coast to contemplate.

❶ ʻŌHIʻA LEHUA
Metrosideros polymorpha
Known for its bright red blossoms and abundance across the island, this flowering evergreen tree has adapted to thrive in Hawaii's volcanic landscapes.
❷ HĀPUʻU TREE FERN
Cibotium menziesii
Known for being the largest tree fern found in Hawaii, this species can reach up to 35 feet tall!
❸ NENE
Branta sandvicensis
The official state bird of Hawaii, the nene has short wings and long legs. It resembles a goose and typically walks more than it flies or swims.
❹ KOAʻE KEA
Phaethon lepturus
Also known as the white-tailed tropicbird, this species is famous for its long tail feathers.
❺ KILAUEA VOLCANO
This is one of the world's most active volcanoes, which also happens to be the youngest on the island of Hawaii. Kilauea regularly spews lava across the park, at times causing damage and forcing the park to close.
KID-FRIENDLY HIKE
Keanakāko'i Crater Trail
This 1-mile path (each way) to Keanakāko'i follows a closed portion of Crater Rim Drive.
❷
❹
❺

HALEAKALĀ

HAWAII • ESTABLISHED 1961 • 52 SQUARE MILES

Next, I made my way to the island of Maui, where I explored Haleakalā's dormant volcano crater high up in the clouds. I hiked into the crater along the Sliding Sands Trail which took me lower and lower, past cinder cones (small, steep-sided volcanic hills) and other volcanic features.

The red, burnt-orange, dark-brown, and black sand created a kaleidoscope of colors. As pretty as it was, the sand beneath my feet was constantly shifting, which made hiking up and out a lot harder than hiking down!

After visiting the crater, I took the Road to Hāna to the Kipahulu section of the park and walked through the lush green rainforest near the coast of the Pacific Ocean where waterfalls flow.

❶ SILVERSWORD
Argyroxiphium sandwicense
Found in and around the Haleakalā crater, this endangered species is known for its sword-like succulent leaves with silver hairs and its flowering stalk, which only blooms once before the plant dies.

❷ 'I'IWI
Drepanis coccinea
Commonly known as honeycreepers, this bright-red bird with black wings has a long, slender, pale-orange bill that it uses to collect nectar from flowers.

❸ WAIMOKU FALLS
This majestic 400-foot-tall waterfall plunges off a sheer cliff in the middle of a tropical rainforest. It can be reached by taking the Pipiwai Trail.

AMERICAN SAMOA

AMERICAN SAMOA • ESTABLISHED 1988 • 21 SQUARE MILES

To get to this park south of the equator, I once again had to fly, this time from Hawaii to the remote island chain of American Samoa, which is known for its rainforests, coral reefs, and dramatic tropical scenery.

These islands are the peaks of ancient underwater volcanoes that rise above the water's surface, which is pretty neat! I enjoyed exploring this tropical paradise, which is covered in lush rainforests from the mountaintops down to the sea—quite a gorgeous combo that's pretty hard to beat.

The park protects three of the islands found here, where many plant and animal species live along the waters of the stunning South Pacific. With its remote location, it's not easy to get to, but boy, is it terrific!

❶ BIRD'S NEST FERN
Asplenium nidus
One of 135 ferns found here, this species' bright-green, often-crinkled fronds grow up to 60 inches long and roll back and collect as they brown, creating what looks like a bird's nest.

❷ CLOWNFISH
Amphiprion ocellaris
The extensive coral reefs surrounding the islands are ideal for this orange-and-white fish, which forms a mutually beneficial relationship with sea anemones, among which it makes its home.

❸ LOWER SAUMA RIDGE
Take a short hike down this ridge through a tropical forest to reach the gorgeous, rocky coastline where tide pools will be at your feet and views of the towering green islands will surround you.

CHANNEL ISLANDS

CALIFORNIA • ESTABLISHED 1980 • 390 SQUARE MILES

Returning to California took two long flights, so I was thrilled to reunite with my camper once I got back to LA! I drove north to Ventura, then got on a ferry to visit Channel Islands National Park, a group of five protected islands that are natural preserves for many species.

On our way, hundreds of dolphins swam in the Pacific Ocean beside the boat, jumping and putting on a show. After an hour and a half, we arrived at Santa Cruz Island—the largest of the five—and got off the boat.

I hiked along the island's north coast, gaining elevation as I walked across wide-open, grassy hills that led to rocky cliffs where land met sea. The trail ended at Potato Harbor, a coastal formation that's so stunning, I didn't want to leave.

❶ ISLAND MALLOW
Malva assurgentiflora
The flowers on this fruiting shrub have five rectangular, pink petals. Island mallow is only found natively growing on the Channel Islands.

❷ ISLAND FOX
Urocyon littoralis
This small fox species is the size of a house cat and descended thousands of years ago from gray foxes. They're known to roam around the islands and have little fear of humans.

❸ POTATO HARBOR
View this potato-shaped harbor from a clifftop, where you can watch waves crash onto its beach, which is surrounded by dramatic rock walls. In the distance, the rest of Santa Cruz Island stretches on for miles to the west.

2

PINNACLES

CALIFORNIA • ESTABLISHED 2013 • 42 SQUARE MILES

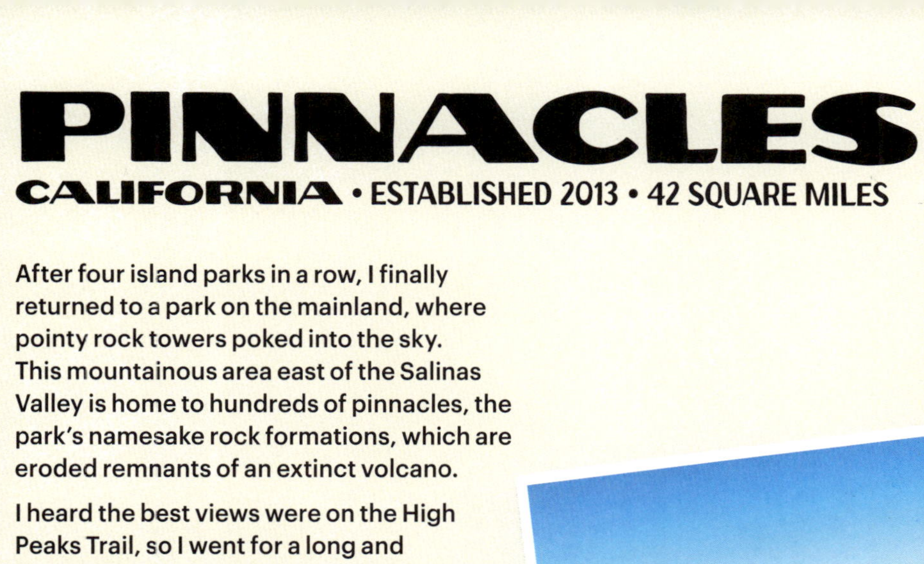

After four island parks in a row, I finally returned to a park on the mainland, where pointy rock towers poked into the sky. This mountainous area east of the Salinas Valley is home to hundreds of pinnacles, the park's namesake rock formations, which are eroded remnants of an extinct volcano.

I heard the best views were on the High Peaks Trail, so I went for a long and challenging hike on this route. The trail took me alongside the lofty pinnacles, as I trekked past countless fascinating rock formations and expansive views of the valley below, while California condors swirled high in the sky above me.

❶ BLUE OAK
Quercus douglasii
California's most drought-tolerant and heat-resistant deciduous oak is the most common oak found here, where it grows on arid slopes.

❷ CALIFORNIA CONDOR
Gymnogyps californianus
The largest land bird in North America with a huge wing span of nearly ten feet, this massive bird can be spotted regularly soaring over the pinnacles, where it scavenges for dead things to eat.

❸ BEAR GULCH CAVE
This talus cave was formed by large rocks falling into an existing canyon, most likely during the last ice age. It's home to hundreds of Townsend's big-eared bats and can be explored by the trail that enters it.

SEQUOIA

CALIFORNIA • ESTABLISHED 1890 • 631 SQUARE MILES

Here, in the southern Sierra Nevada, you'll find forested mountain terrain that's home to the giant sequoia, the world's largest tree. Walking through the Giant Forest is quite astounding, as the trees are so tall and wide you can barely fit them into view. Even when I was standing in front of General Sherman (the biggest tree in the world!), I could hardly believe what was in front of me.

Sequoia has so much to see, as it's also home to rugged foothills, deep canyons, and Mount Whitney, the highest peak in the lower 48 states, at 14,505 feet high. After a fabulous day exploring, I watched the sunset at Beetle Rock, where warm colors set the west edge of the park, and the San Joaquin Valley below, totally aglow.

Darkness began to settle in as a small, brown-and-white owl dove from a tree and started to circle the sky above where I sat near a few other people. I overheard someone say, "Sequoia has to be one of the best of California's nine national parks, don't you think?" And although I didn't hear the answer, I agreed.

❶ GIANT SEQUOIA

Sequoiadendron giganteum

Growing on the western slopes of the Sierra Nevada mountain range, this coniferous tree with its notable reddish-orange bark is the largest tree species on Earth. The trees can grow up to 300 feet tall, nearly 30 feet wide, and sometimes live for 3,000 years or more.

❷ WHITE FIR

Abies concolor

Growing in mountainous areas of mixed-conifer forests, this tree outnumbers the larger sequoia across the park.

❸ NORTHERN PYGMY OWL

Glaucidium californicum

This tiny owl likes to perch at the top of the tallest tree it can find and issue territorial calls that sound like a series of high-pitched toots.

❹ SPOTTED TOWHEE

Pipilo maculatus

A large, multicolored sparrow that's known for hopping between shrubs and leaf-covered areas on the ground.

❺ MORO ROCK

This enormous granite dome rock formation at the center of the park has a stairway carved into it, so you can hike to its top. The impressive views showcase Sequoia's mountainous, forested terrain in all directions.

KID-FRIENDLY HIKE

Congress Trail

This paved, 2.7-mile round-trip lollipop-shaped trail takes you through some of the most stunning sequoia groves in the park.

3

KINGS CANYON

CALIFORNIA • ESTABLISHED 1940 • 722 SQUARE MILES

If you want more giant trees, this park right next to Sequoia is also home to these famous, massive trees in a place called Grant Grove, which includes the General Grant Tree, the second-largest tree in the world.

To explore more, I drove further into the park. It felt like I was making my way toward the center of the Earth. The park road weaves down past huge rock walls and descends thousands of feet in elevation. This glacier-carved valley is actually deeper than the Grand Canyon, if you can believe it!

After seeing impressive views of the canyon as I drove, I stopped at Zumwalt Meadow near the end of the park road and walked along the trail that starts there.

While I only got to hike for a little while, I learned that so much of what this park has to offer exists along trails in the backcountry, far from any roads, where the allure of the Sierra Nevada calls. I promised myself I'd return and backpack, some other year.

❶

❶ PONDEROSA PINE

Pinus ponderosa

This large pine tree is widely distributed across mountainous regions in the Western United States. At Kings Canyon, it greatly outnumbers the sequoia, as it grows in areas across the park.

❷ CRIMSON COLUMBINE

Aquilegia formosa

This fancy-looking wildflower is reddish-orange in color and is often pollinated by hummingbirds.

❸ YELLOW-BELLIED MARMOT

Marmota flaviventris

Commonly seen in open meadows and on rocky slopes, this species is highly social and lives in burrows with up to 20 others.

❹ MULE DEER

Odocoileus hemionus

Found across the Western states, this deer has a black-tipped tail and is named for its large, mule-like ears. Impressively, males shed and regrow their antlers each year.

❺ ZUMWALT MEADOW

This serene, grassy meadow along the Kings River brings a sense of calm to all those who visit it, as its openness greatly contrasts with the jagged, rocky nature of other parts of the park.

KID-FRIENDLY HIKE

Roaring River Falls Trail

This short, paved 0.3-mile trail (round-trip) leads to a powerful waterfall.

YOSEMITE

CALIFORNIA • ESTABLISHED 1890 • 1,187 SQUARE MILES

I drove north to visit the crown jewel of the Sierra Nevada mountain range and arguably California's most astonishing park: Yosemite. Witnessing the world-famous valley for the first time—with its sheer granite monoliths, waterfalls so tall they seemed to descend from the sky, and evergreen trees in groves galore—made me feel as if I'd discovered heaven on Earth.

After appreciating the vista at Tunnel View, I headed into the valley, peering up at the massive sheer rock face of El Capitan, which loomed high above me. I took a short walk to see Bridalveil Fall, a wispy water cascade, and then embarked on a longer hike to the top of Yosemite Falls, which plunges 2,425 feet from a granite cliff's edge.

Later in the day, as the crowds began to thin, I paused on Sentinel Bridge to soak up the fantastic view of the world-famous rock formation Half Dome, in the reflection of the Merced River. I thought about nature's glory, and how so many people are too far removed from it nowadays, with their faces stuck behind digital screens.

A young park ranger who looked to be my age approached where I stood and paused to enjoy the view with me, before offering a bit of trivia. "Did you know Yosemite was the first place the US government set aside to preserve, in 1864?" he asked me. "Thank goodness they did, or all this beauty could've been lost." He wished me a great visit and then continued on his way.

❶ SNOW PLANT
Sarcodes sanguinea
A bright-red plant that grows on the forest floor in spring and often pushes up through snow, this species cannot photosynthesize, so it pulls nourishment from fungi in the soil.
❷ MOUNTAIN PRIDE
Penstemon newberryi
Known for showy, bright-magenta tubular flowers that protrude from its shrublike base, this plant can be found growing in high-elevation, rocky habitats in the park.
❸ PACIFIC FISHER
Martes pennanti
This carnivorous mammal has a long brown body and is a superb climber. It doesn't eat fish as its name suggests, but instead is known for being one of the few animals to chow down on porcupines.
❹ PEREGRINE FALCON
Falco peregrinus
During high speed dives, this species can reach over 200 miles per hour, making it the fastest animal on Earth. They nest on the granite cliffs, domes, and spires found in the park.
❺ HALF DOME
An icon of Yosemite, this enormous rock formation dominates the eastern end of the valley, where it reaches 8,846 feet high. Three sides are smooth and round, while a fourth has a sheer cliff face, giving it the appearance of a dome cut in half.
KID-FRIENDLY HIKE
Mirror Lake Trail
This is a 2-mile (round-trip) paved trail that leads to Mirror Lake. The lake is fullest in spring and early summer, when it boasts stunning reflections of the nearby cliffs.
❺
❷

LASSEN VOLCANIC

CALIFORNIA • ESTABLISHED 1916 • 166 SQUARE MILES

I left the Sierra Nevada mountains behind as I drove my camper to new ones, further north in California: the Cascades. This mountain range's southernmost volcano, Lassen Peak, looms large against the sky here.

Because the park road climbs so high, I was able to hike to the volcano's peak, taking in inspiring views of other mountains from the top. From 1914 to 1921, Lassen—the largest plug dome volcano in the world—released a series of eruptions, leading to its protection as a national park.

This park is one of the only areas in the world where all four types of volcanoes can be found, as it boasts shield, cinder cone, and composite volcanoes, too. With gorgeous lakes, stunning volcanic peaks, bubbling hot springs, and lush, green wilderness, this underrated park is a natural playground to wander through.

❶

❸

❶ COPPER MOSS

Haplodontium tehamense

Only found in the park growing on high, northern-facing slopes, this rare moss is shiny light-green in color, and is known for its bulbous fruiting bodies.

❷ OSPREY

Pandion haliaetus

This large, predatory bird can be identified by its dark brown wings and white belly. It feeds almost exclusively on fish, so keep an eye out for it near water.

❸ BUMPASS HELL

Spanning 16 acres, this geothermally active part of the park boasts hot springs, fumaroles, and boiling mudpots. You can walk along boardwalks next to the thermal features to get an up-close look.

2

1

REDWOOD

CALIFORNIA • ESTABLISHED 1968 • 206 SQUARE MILES

Along California's northern coast, the tallest trees in the world grow high toward the sky. These tall, skinny trees aren't as wide as sequoias, but they reach greater heights.

Redwood National Park, along with three adjacent state parks, protect these incredible coastal trees, which grow in this foggy, temperate rainforest.

This region along the Pacific Coast in North America is the only place where these huge old-growth trees take root. I got to see the trees up close, hiking in the Tall Trees Grove, where the tops of the trees stretched so high, they disappeared into the misty fog above.

Later in the day, the clouds let up, and I was rewarded with clear skies and sunshine as I went for a walk along gorgeous Gold Bluffs Beach. 40 miles of rugged coastline is also protected here!

❶ COAST REDWOOD

Sequoia sempervirens

The tallest living tree on Earth, this evergreen species can grow up to 380 feet tall and live for over 2,000 years! The national and state parks here protect nearly 45 percent of all the redwoods that remain.

❷ RIVER OTTER

Lontra canadensis

Look for this mammal poking its head out of creeks and rivers or traveling on land to reach its burrow that's usually close to the water's edge.

❸ TRILLIUM FALLS

Hike down an easy 0.5-mile trail to reach this small cascading waterfall which flows amid an old-growth forest of redwoods, maples, trillium flowers, and ferns.

CRATER LAKE

OREGON • ESTABLISHED 1902 • 286 SQUARE MILES

With my tour of California's nine national parks complete, I drove into Southern Oregon, arriving at the edge of spectacular Crater Lake, the deepest lake in our country. This striking, bright-blue lake's crystal-clear water is fed only by rain and snowmelt, as the lake exists in the hollowed-out caldera of an extinct volcano, Mount Mazama.

I circled Rim Drive in the camper, getting to see the lake from various viewpoints along the caldera's edge. Watchman Peak was a great spot to climb up to enjoy epic views of Wizard Island, and Phantom Ship Overlook was well worth the stop to see an eerie rock formation in the lake that looks like a floating ghost ship.

I ended the day by trekking down a steep trail to Cleetwood Cove, the only place where you can swim in the lake. Seeking a thrill, I jumped off a small cliff into the freezing, cobalt-blue water, submerging myself in the power of nature's creation.

❶

❸

❷

❶ WHITEBARK PINE

Pinus albicaulis

This tough, long-living tree species can tolerate severe conditions and high elevations. It plays an important role in creating and sustaining plant communities.

❷ VOLCANIC DAISY

Erigeron elegantulus

The lavender-colored petals of this flower encircle a bright yellow center. It's found growing throughout the park on rocky, volcanic soils.

❸ CLARK'S NUTCRACKER

Nucifraga columbiana

The cones of the whitebark pine are regularly opened by this bird, which extracts its seeds for food. This process spreads seeds around, which can lead to new trees growing.

❹ SNOWSHOE HARE

Lepus americanus

This hare gets its name from its large hind feet, which prevent it from sinking into the snow. In the summer, its fur is brown, but in winter it becomes a camouflaged white, which allows it to blend into Crater Lake's surroundings, no matter the season.

❺ WIZARD ISLAND

This island on the west side of the lake is a volcanic cinder cone, formed by later eruptions after Mount Mazama collapsed. Its top reaches 755 feet above the lake's surface. During the summer, you can take a boat tour to gain access to the island.

KID-FRIENDLY HIKE

Pinnacles Valley Trail

This easy 0.8-mile (round-trip) trail takes you along the rim of the valley to see the pinnacles: spires of hardened volcanic matter that have eroded.

OLYMPIC

WASHINGTON • ESTABLISHED 1938 • 1,442 SQUARE MILES

The Evergreen State welcomed me with shades of emerald as I arrived on the Olympic Peninsula, which is home to this incredibly diverse park. Here you can explore temperate rainforests, glacial valleys, mountainous peaks, scenic beaches, and stunning lakes.

I decided to backpack the Hoh River Trail, trekking through a dense, moss-covered old-growth rainforest, where the tall trees and plants are every possible shade of green.

Along the way, I came across a large, male Roosevelt elk who was huffing as he pushed his muzzle into the ground. "What're you looking for?" I asked him, knowing he couldn't answer me, but wondering aloud all the same. He made a bellowing sound, but he didn't lift his large, antler-covered head to look at me. As I watched him for a bit longer (from a safe distance) I realized he was nibbling on some white mushrooms that had burst forth from the moist ground.

After hiking along the Hoh River for over 13 miles, I started to gain elevation, climbing up into the Olympic Mountains until the trail ended beside the awe-inspiring Blue Glacier.

Standing before this huge icy glacier at the base of Mount Olympus after pushing through so many miles of lush rainforest felt otherworldly. I savored the view for as long as I could, then made the 18-mile trek back to the camper at the rainforest's edge. I cleaned myself up, then drove to Third Beach.

Once parked at the trailhead, I went on a 1.4-mile hike through the woods to get to the coast. I arrived at a sandy beach sprinkled with towering rock formations where waves crashed ashore. I lingered until the sun set, letting the warm glow wash me in its glory.

❺

❶ ANGEL WING MUSHROOM

Pleurocybella porrigens
The bright-white, delicate fruiting bodies of this mushroom look like an angel's wings. It grows in forests and works to digest the rotting and decaying wood of conifer trees. While some animals eat them, they're considered poisonous to humans.

❷ GLITTERING WOOD-MOSS

Hylocomium splendens
Also known as the stairstep moss, this species can be found growing all over other plants in the temperate rainforest, where it produces green, feathery fronds that grow in steps.

❸ ROOSEVELT ELK

Cervus canadensis roosevelti
This large elk can weigh up to 1,200 pounds and thrives in the temperate rainforests of the Pacific Northwest. It feeds on herbaceous plants and is also known to eat ferns, blueberries, and mushrooms.

❹ OLYMPIC CHIPMUNK

Tamias amoenus caurinus
Found only on the Olympic Peninsula, this chipmunk species can be spotted darting along the forest floor, foraging for nuts, seeds, and berries.

❺ LAKE CRESCENT

This large, brilliant-blue lake was formed during the last ice age by glaciers. Its crescent shape can be witnessed from the top of the challenging Mount Storm King trail.

KID-FRIENDLY HIKE

Hall of Mosses Trail
This 0.8-mile (round-trip) gravel loop trail weaves through a wonderland of moss, trees, and ferns.

MOUNT RAINIER

WASHINGTON • ESTABLISHED 1899 • 369 SQUARE MILES

Gorgeous Mount Rainier dominates the sky in Western Washington, showing off its glacier-covered surface and serving as a timeless beacon to all who gaze upon it. It's the most topographically prominent mountain in the lower 48, which means it reaches noticeable, extremely high elevations compared to the surrounding terrain. No wonder so many people shout with glee when they spot it for the first time!

While it can be seen from Seattle and elsewhere, you have to head into the park to experience its true magic. In the park you can explore the alpine tundra, wildflower meadows, and old-growth forests that surround this icy volcano.

To see Rainier up close, I headed to the Sunrise area and hiked the Mount Fremont Lookout Trail, which climbs along a ridge to an old fire lookout. The views of the mountain are absolutely stunning from here. You can even see many of the glaciers' details—deep crevasses, rock debris, and meltwater flowing out from where the ice ends.

❶ AVALANCHE LILY

Erythronium montanum

Often the first wildflower to appear after the snow melts, this species can be recognized by its white petals and yellow center.

❷ COMMON RED PAINTBRUSH

Castilleja miniata

This subalpine wildflower is commonly found in the park above 5,000 feet. Its lance-shaped leaves are bright red in color, appearing as if they have been dipped in paint.

❸ AMERICAN MARTEN

Martes americana

Found in the coniferous forests that surround the mountain, this species has large furry feet, prominent ears, retractable claws, and a narrow, foxlike face.

❹ HOARY MARMOT

Marmota caligata

Often seen clambering around subalpine regions of the park, eating meadow vegetation, this species is the largest member of the squirrel family and is known for its shrill whistle call, which warns against potential predators.

❺ TAHOMA

Called Mount Ranier (or its native name Tahoma), this active stratovolcano is the most glaciated peak in the lower 48 and ascends 14,410 feet. It spawns five major rivers and is encircled by the magnificent Wonderland Trail, which showcases the park's exquisite landscapes.

KID-FRIENDLY HIKE

Skyline Trail to Myrtle Falls

Head to the Paradise area of the park to hike this 1-mile (round-trip) paved trail that leads to a lovely view of the 60-foot waterfall with Rainier in the background.

NORTH CASCADES

WASHINGTON • ESTABLISHED 1968 • 789 SQUARE MILES

I drove north through the Emerald City of Seattle and arrived in the North Cascades, where rugged mountains and stunning lakes abound—these are known as the American Alps. The road that crosses the park climbs past turquoise Diablo Lake, which has a great lookout that's worth a stop.

After driving along the road to get more alpine views, I turned back at Washington Pass, then began the 9-mile round-trip hike up to the Thornton Lakes, where jagged mountain peaks rise behind bright-blue lakes surrounded by towering evergreens.

Tired from my full day, I camped overnight, then checked in at the visitor center the next morning to ask for a recommendation on what to do. "This might not be Glacier National Park," a young female park ranger with brilliant red hair told me, "but we've got more glaciers here than anywhere else in the lower 48 states. If you want to see glaciers, this is the place to be."

I took her advice, which was to head into the southern section of the park to tackle the hike up to Cascade Pass, where I could see the kinds of glaciers she was talking about. Trekking up dozens of switchbacks was worth it, as reaching the mountain pass revealed mountains covered in glaciers as far as the eye could see.

A couple of mountain goats sauntered by in the valley below as I savored the view, a grizzled old one even stopping to stare at me for a few seconds, almost as if it was saying hello.

❶ BRACKEN FERN
Pteridium aquilinum
Often found covering the park's forest floor, this fern thrives in the low light and high moisture of the North Cascades.

❷ ALPINE LARCH
Larix lyallii
This deciduous conifer tree grows at high altitudes across the park and is famous for turning bright shades of gold and losing its needles every autumn.

❸ WOLVERINE
Gulo gulo
After nearly being hunted to extinction in the early 1900s, this thick-furred species has returned to the park and can be found across its mountainous, snowy terrain.

❹ MOUNTAIN GOAT
Oreamnos americanus
Known for their strong muscular legs, sturdy hooves, and compact bodies, with thick white hair and wool, this species can travel across steep mountainous terrain. Both males and females have beards and horns.

❺ CASCADE PASS
This 5,392-foot mountain pass is one of the most popular day hikes in the park, offering stunning views of the northern Cascade Range in every direction.

KID-FRIENDLY HIKE
Thunder Knob Trail
A moderate 3.4-mile loop, this trail is suitable for children who enjoy a bit of a challenge. It offers gorgeous views of Diablo Lake and the surrounding mountains.

3

GLACIER BAY

ALASKA • ESTABLISHED 1980 • 5,125 SQUARE MILES

The Last Frontier called me north as I flew from Seattle to Juneau, then took another short flight to the small town of Gustavus, the gateway to Glacier Bay.

I had an incredible time on a day-long cruise into the bay, where I spotted tufted puffins flying about, sea otters floating on their backs, grizzlies clambering along the rocky shoreline, and even orcas breaching the cold water's surface to greet the day.

The cruise's highlight was when our boat pulled up next to John Hopkins Glacier—an enormous bright-blue tidewater glacier—just as chunks of ice broke off and plunged into the bay below with loud thuds and splashes.

❶ FIREWEED

Chamaenerion angustifolium

A tall perennial wildflower that's abundant across Alaska, this species is famous for its bright-pink petals, which bloom from the bottom up, sometimes reaching six feet tall.

❷ ORCA

Orcinus orca

Also called the killer whale, this striking black-and-white marine mammal is the largest member of the oceanic dolphin family and hunts for a variety of fish, sharks, and marine mammals in tight-knit pods.

❸ GLACIER BAY

Surrounded by the Fairweather Range, Glacier Bay has many branches, inlets, lagoons, and islands that are home to abundant wildlife and more than 50 tidewater and terrestrial glaciers, with thousands more in the nearby peaks.

WRANGELL-ST. ELIAS

ALASKA • ESTABLISHED 1980 • 20,587 SQUARE MILES

The largest national park in America, Wrangell-St. Elias is a wilderness wonderland that stretches from the sea to the 18,008-foot peak of Mount St. Elias, the second tallest mountain in the country. Four mountain ranges come together here, and the landscape has been shaped not only by glaciers, but by volcanoes and plate tectonics, too.

I explored this massive park by heading into the old mining town of Kennecott, where rich copper deposits were mined from 1903 to 1938.

From here, I walked past the town's many abandoned red wooden buildings and hiked the Root Glacier Trail, passing through evergreens before reaching the huge stretch of ice. I was even able to hike on the glacier itself, my first time ever walking across one of these incredible icy formations!

❶ ARCTIC LUPINE

Lupinus arcticus

A tall, purple-blue wildflower that blooms early in the summer and shows off up to 30 flowers at a time. It's a member of the legume family and may hybridize with other lupines when they grow beside one another.

❷ DALL SHEEP

Ovis dalli

These white, wild sheep can be found foraging on lichens and other plants along rocky ridges in the park. Males have thick, curling horns that grow annually from spring through fall.

❸ ROOT GLACIER

Stretching 15 miles down from Regal Mountain and terminating near the town of Kennecott, this is the most accessible glacier in the park.

3

KENAI FJORDS

ALASKA • ESTABLISHED 1980 • 1,047 SQUARE MILES

With the town of Seward as my base, I explored this fascinating park, where mountains, ice, and sea meet. I went on a spectacular 9-mile hike on the Harding Icefield Trail, which weaves through forests and passes by the lower-lying Exit Glacier.

Dazzling mountain views surrounded me as I climbed, continuously becoming more epic until I made it to the enormous icefield, where I had to be careful not to slide. A blanket of ice and snow seemed to go on forever from here, and even though I tried, I couldn't spot where the white ended in the mountains beyond.

The next day, I left the peninsula behind on a guided cruise, our boat coasting through Resurrection Bay, where we saw humpback whales breaching the surface and puffins nesting on towering rock islands. We sailed through the fjords and got up close to Aialik Glacier, spotting lots of gigantic chunks of ice that had broken off it and were now floating in the sea.

On our way back toward Seward, I spotted a humpback swimming close to the surface as I stood next to our tour guide and we watched in awe. I decided to ask him a question. "What's your favorite part about this place?"

The whale's giant eye blinked at us and then disappeared under the surface before the guide answered me, saying: "Getting to see that look of excitement on everyone's face."

❶ SITKA SPRUCE

Picea sitchensis

The dominant tree found in Kenai's temperate rainforest, this coniferous species can live for over 700 years and is known for being one of the world's tallest.

❷ SITKA VALERIAN

Valeriana sitchensis

Known to thrive in moist mountain forests and subalpine meadows, this perennial herb produces a tall stem with white, pink-tinged flowers.

❸ HORNED PUFFIN

Fratercula corniculata

Often seen nesting on small fjord islands, this diving bird swims underwater to catch fish.

❹ HUMPBACK WHALE

Megaptera novaeangliae

This species uses the large baleen plates lining the roof of its mouth to strain out seawater as it swallows loads of krill. Females are larger, growing up to 49 feet long and weighing up to 35 tons!

❺ HARDING ICEFIELD

Receiving over 400 inches of snow each year, this is the largest icefield in the United States and spawns over 40 different glaciers.

KID-FRIENDLY HIKE

Exit Glacier Trail

This relatively easy 2.2-mile loop trail takes you close to the edge of Exit Glacier, a huge, brilliant-blue sheath of ice that pushes down the mountainside from the Harding Icefield.

3

KATMAI

ALASKA • ESTABLISHED 1980 • 6,395 SQUARE MILES

To get to this park on the Alaska Peninsula, I had to fly in on a small plane, because this designated wilderness area can't be accessed by road. Named after its centerpiece stratovolcano, Mount Katmai, this park is famous for its brown bears and the Valley of Ten Thousand Smokes, which is filled with ash flow from the largest volcanic eruption of the 20th century, in 1912.

At Brooks Falls, I saw a large group of brown bears up close from a viewing platform and watched in awe as they fed on the sockeye salmon they caught from the Brooks River.

❶

❷

❶ NORTHERN GERANIUM

Geranium erianthum

Light purple in color, this wildflower can be found in the meadows, forests, and tundras of Katmai between June and August.

❷ BROWN BEAR

Ursus arctos

The Alaska brown bear is incredibly large and requires a very high intake of calories, eating up to 90 pounds of food per day to store fat for winter hibernation. There are an estimated 2,200 brown bears living in the park.

❸ BROOKS FALLS

This six-foot high waterfall bisects the Brooks River where it flows between two lakes, causing salmon to get stuck as they migrate upstream, making it the perfect place for bears to come and feast.

LAKE CLARK

ALASKA • ESTABLISHED 1980 • 6,297 SQUARE MILES

I hopped aboard another small plane and headed north to get to my next park. This park is another immense Alaskan wilderness, where there are rainforests along the coast, glaciers and glacial lakes to witness, rivers full of salmon to feed bear populations, and two volcanoes standing tall—with Mount Redoubt still active.

Since this park is named after it, I decided to kayak out onto Lake Clark. I paddled to Tommy Island from Port Alsworth, enjoying all the natural beauty I could see. Being in the middle of such a wild landscape—where mountains, lakes, rivers, forests, glaciers, volcanoes, and tundra all come together to create something so beautiful and serene—felt pretty special to me.

❷

❶

❶ BLACK SPRUCE
Picea mariana
This species is very durable and well-adapted to cold environments. With dark green needles, hairy-looking twigs, and purplish seed cones, its appearance is quite memorable.

❷ HARLEQUIN DUCK
Histrionicus histrionicus
This small diving duck is known for its slate blue-gray feathers and distinctive markings on its head, neck, and sides. It spends most of its life along the coast, but moves inland to breed in fast-moving streams.

❸ LAKE CLARK
Ringed by mountains, this 42-mile-long lake is a stunning turquoise color, and serves as the central point from which to explore the park.

3

DENALI

ALASKA • ESTABLISHED 1917 • 9,492 SQUARE MILES

To get to the most iconic park in Alaska, I returned to Anchorage and drove to the heart of the state, where our country's tallest peak lay in wait.

Here, the Alaska Range reaches high in the sky with one enormous white, glaciated peak after another, with Denali standing the tallest among them all. Following the Denali Park Road, I immersed myself in this wild terrain, where boreal forest, alpine tundra, glacial valleys, and snowcapped mountains spread out as far as the eye could see.

This wilderness is the kind of place you dream about, a place where there are so many vast, beautiful layers of untouched, natural terrain. The landscapes almost seem unreal.

Where the park's road dead-ends near Kantishna, I paused next to a stream and watched in awe as a herd of caribou clambered over a nearby hillside, coming to the water's edge to gather for a drink.

With Denali serving as a magnificent backdrop behind them, I savored the scene before me, but at the same time, I worried that we weren't doing enough to protect this environment and the other places in our country like it.

A stray caribou wandered over, stopped ten feet from me, and looked at me directly as if it could read my mind. I took its appearance and acknowledgment of me as a good sign, so I decided to speak my thoughts aloud. "Hopefully more and more people will be inspired by the wonders of nature to help protect these lands. And maybe the power of nature itself will also find a way to deal with the challenges of climate change."

❶ ALPINE FORGET-ME-NOT
Myosotis alpestris
Alaska's state flower, this species blooms bright-blue and grows on rocky, mountainous terrain.
❷ LINGONBERRY
Vaccinium vitis-idaea
This small evergreen shrub is native to boreal forests. It grows commonly throughout the park from lowland bogs to high alpine tundra, offering its edible tart red berries to those who pass by.
❸ CARIBOU
Rangifer tarandus
Large herds of this reindeer species are commonly seen in the park. It's known for both its males and females growing large antlers, which can be up to three feet tall or more.
❹ GOLDEN EAGLE
Aquila chrysaetos
The park boasts a high number of this powerful bird of prey, which migrates to the park and nests here, with scientists tracking their movements.
❺ DENALI
The highest mountain in North America at 20,310 feet, Denali rises dramatically above the Alaskan Range and the wilderness it's a part of. Its name in the native Alaskan language translates to "the high one."
KID-FRIENDLY HIKE
Horseshoe Lake Trail
A moderately challenging hike that's best suited for older children, this 2.1-mile loop trail circles around a peaceful lake.
❺
❹
❶
❷

3

KOBUK VALLEY

ALASKA • ESTABLISHED 1980 • 2,736 SQUARE MILES

The Arctic Circle called me even further north, as I flew to a remote part of Northwestern Alaska, where another roadless park awaited. This was my fortieth park!

The Kobuk River meanders through this vast untamed wilderness, flowing across the southern section of this protected terrain. Many visitors choose to explore by traveling on rafts along the river's waterways, but I decided to fly in onto the sand dunes aboard a small plane instead.

I hiked across the huge dunes, fascinated by how far they stretched onward, between the boreal forests and the treeless Arctic tundra further north.

Thousands of caribou migrate across these dunes in enormous herds, and although I didn't spy any while I walked, I noticed their tracks, which were still imprinted upon the sand.

❶ KOBUK LOCOWEED

Oxytropis kobukensis

A member of the pea family that dazzles with magenta flowers, this species is found only in the park, growing on sparsely vegetated dunes.

❷ CANADA LYNX

Lynx canadensis

This wild cat is identified by its triangular ears, which have pointy black tufts of hair, its dense golden-hued fur, and its powerful legs, which help it hunt for snowshoe hares.

❸ GREAT KOBUK SAND DUNES

The largest active sand dunes in the Arctic, created during the last ice age, these dunes cover more than 25 square miles and are very slowly being reclaimed by vegetation.

GATES OF THE ARCTIC

ALASKA • ESTABLISHED 1980 • 13,238 SQUARE MILES

I headed to America's northernmost park next. My eighth and final park in Alaska is known for remote, rugged landscapes that stretch on endlessly in the Arctic. I had a bush pilot fly me into the southwestern part of the park, where I got dropped off on a gravel bar along the Upper Noatak River.

From here, I began hiking into the vast, untouched wilderness, where the peaks of the Brooks Range loom large and wild rivers cross the land.

I backpacked across Arctic tundra, walked through boreal forest, and camped next to scenic, still lakes that were so quiet I could hear the beating of my own heart as I savored the peaceful scenery, all while basking in the glow of the never-ending midnight sun.

❷

❶ GREEN ALDER

Alnus alnobetula

A small tree with shiny green leaves, it thrives in this challenging ecosystem due to its resilience and ability to make the poor soils of the Arctic work for it. This species can regrow after sustaining avalanche damage.

❷ MUSKOX

Ovibos moschatus

This large, hoofed mammal is known for its thick brown coat, musky smell, and the elegant-looking horns that curve from its forehead toward its face.

❸ MOUNT IGIKPAK

The tallest mountain in the park at 8,276 feet, its jagged, rocky surfaces puncture the sky where it dominates the terrain near the source of the Noatak River.

3

GLACIER

MONTANA • ESTABLISHED 1910 • 1,583 SQUARE MILES

After weeks in Alaska, I flew back to Seattle and picked up the camper to continue my adventure. The Crown of the Continent called me to northwest Montana, where Big Sky Country is dramatic and grand.

I entered Glacier along the famed Going-to-the-Sun Road. This windy route climbs up mountains and rocky cliffs that dominate the land. As I drove, the majesty of this park was revealed—carved valleys, high peaks, alpine meadows, melting glaciers, and stunning lakes were all spread across this region of the Rockies that straddles the Continental Divide.

I continued onward to the Many Glacier area, where I hiked the Grinnell Glacier Trail, smiling from ear to ear because of the fantastic views. The bright-turquoise Grinnell Lake shone in the sun underneath Angel Wing mountain, as small waterfalls cascaded beneath me while I climbed higher.

❶ **BEARGRASS**

Xerophyllum tenax

This species is actually a wildflower that's known for its large, fluffy balls of white blossoms. It grows up to five feet tall and is found across the park.

❷ **GLACIER LILY**

Erythronium grandiflorum

Also known as the yellow avalanche lily, this delicate wildflower is often found growing along the edge of melting snow.

At trail's end, I sat beside the icy-blue Upper Grinnell Lake, which is below Grinnell Glacier, and took a rest. The glacier on the mountainside looked so much smaller than in the historic pictures I'd seen.

Just then, a herd of bighorn sheep stormed down a cliff and spread out along the lake's edge. Those of us gathered watched in wonder, frozen. I felt a tugging on my backpack and turned around to find a young girl with curly dark hair standing next to her parents, who were still distracted by the bighorn sheep.

"Did you know there used to be over a hundred glaciers here?" she asked, sharing the fact she must have just learned, "but now there's only twenty-five left because our climate's changing. Will we be able to save the rest?"

"If we work together and can encourage others to do more to protect the environment, I have hope," I whispered, which brought a smile to her face.

3 BIGHORN SHEEP

Ovis canadensis

With large curling horns on either side of their heads that can weigh up to 30 pounds as a pair (on males), this species travels in herds, climbing steep terrain to feed on grasses and shrubs.

4 BEAVER

Castor canadensis

The largest rodent in North America, this species can chew through wood. They build their lodges with sticks and logs, constructing dams on rivers and streams.

5 GRINNELL GLACIER

Resting on the north flank of Mount Gould at around 7,000 feet, this is one of the most photographed glaciers in the park. In 1850, the glacier measured 710 acres, whereas recent estimates put it around 115 acres.

KID-FRIENDLY HIKE

Hidden Lake Overlook

This moderate 2.7-mile (round-trip) trail leads to an overlook where views of Hidden Lake and Bearhat Mountain will leave you breathless.

YELLOWSTONE

WYOMING (MONTANA, AND IDAHO) • ESTABLISHED 1872 • 3,472 SQUARE MILES

America's first national park is so unusual it feels like a land of make-believe. Sitting atop a dormant, ancient volcano, Yellowstone is home to more geysers and hot springs than anywhere else on Earth.

I visited the Upper Geyser Basin, where I walked past hot spring pools of blue, orange, and green and got to see the world-famous geyser, Old Faithful, erupt. It shoots huge sprays of hot water high into the air at regular intervals, according to its own unique clock.

The Grand Canyon of the Yellowstone was my next stop. It's an impressive canyon of multicolored rhyolite rock that's been altered by hydrothermal activity and carved by the rushing waters of the Yellowstone River and its powerful waterfalls.

As I drove south, I stumbled upon a bison herd crossing the road, so I pulled over to watch them and snap some photos at a safe distance. My cell phone rang, and I saw that my mom was calling. I kept watching the bison as I answered and told her about my adventures.

"What're you going to do when you're done?" she asked, bringing up a question I didn't know how to answer. "The future's still quickly approaching, honey, even in a place as timeless as Yellowstone," she said. I thought about my future as the bison left, imagining all the things that could come next.

❶ YELLOWSTONE SULFUR FLOWER

Eriogonum umbellatum cladophorum

This species is native to the park and only found in the Firehole River drainage area. With bright-yellow flowers and hairy, gray leaves, it grows on mild geothermal terrain.

❷ LODGEPOLE PINE

Pinus contorta

The most common tree found in the park, this species does not enjoy the shade, and branches left without sunlight will wither and fall off.

❸ PRONGHORN

Antilocapra americana

In the early 1800s, this species was found in the millions across the American West. It is the fastest land mammal on the continent.

❹ AMERICAN BISON

Bison bison

Yellowstone preserves the most important herd in the US. Here, bison roam freely in the thousands. Known for their dark brown color, fluffy faces, short horns, and humped backs, bison are an American icon.

❺ GRAND PRISMATIC SPRING

A multicolored pool of blue, green, yellow, and orange that's the largest hot spring in the country, Grand Prismatic is ethereal. The vivid colors are created by microbial mats made up of bacteria and other microorganisms too small to see.

KID-FRIENDLY HIKE

Mammoth Hot Springs Terraces

Explore the travertine terraces (large, step-like sections of limestone) that climb up the hillside in shades of white, orange, and yellow. You can walk up to 2.5 miles (round-trip) around this fascinating geothermal area.

❸

GRAND TETON

WYOMING • ESTABLISHED 1929 • 484 SQUARE MILES

About an hour's drive directly south of Yellowstone, another park awaits, with magnificent mountains and crystal-clear lakes. As soon as I entered the park's boundaries, the all-impressive Teton Range appeared through the camper's windows, touching the sky with its pointed granite peaks.

I drove further into the park, where the Grand Teton rose high above me to an astounding 13,775 feet.

I trekked across the Valley Trail, and as I approached the edge of Phelps Lake, I came across a male moose ambling along the route. I was far enough away that he didn't notice me, so I stood still and watched this large, powerful creature as he moved confidently along in his wild home.

1 QUAKING ASPEN
Populus tremuloides
Growing throughout the park near water and on mountain slopes, this tall tree has smooth pale bark with black splotches. The glossy green leaves dance and quake when the wind blows.

2 MOOSE
Alces alces
The largest member of the deer family, this species thrives in cooler, boreal, and temperate forests where it feeds on a variety of vegetation. Males are known for their broad antlers, which spread out from their heads in dignified racks.

3 JENNY LAKE
This lake is situated in the heart of the park, right underneath the mountains, their impressive façades reflected perfectly in its still waters. If you only have time for one stop in the park, this is where you should go.

GREAT BASIN

NEVADA • ESTABLISHED 1986 • 121 SQUARE MILES

After hours of driving through Wyoming and Utah, I arrived at my next park right across the border of Nevada.

A stunning route called Scenic Drive took me into the park, climbing over 4,000 feet and passing through a variety of terrain as Wheeler Peak grew larger on the skyline.

Great Basin is remote, but it's worth visiting to see ancient trees, fascinating caves, and dark skies without light pollution for superb stargazing.

I hiked the Bristlecone Pine Trail, getting to see groves of these super old trees up close. I continued onto the Glacier Trail, hiking to the base of Wheeler Peak, where the state's only glacier remains in any icy pocket of rock.

❶ GREAT BASIN BRISTLECONE PINE

Pinus longaeva

The world's longest-living tree, reaching ages up to 4,900 years, this species grows at high elevations on rocky terrain. It grows slowly and adapts to strenuous conditions, resulting in a gnarled and stunted shape.

❷ GREAT BASIN RATTLESNAKE

Crotalus lutosus

This venomous reptile can be found in dry, barren areas, basking in the sun to regulate its temperature. If you see a snake that's pale gray-brown with dark splotches and hear a rattle, stay away!

❸ WHEELER PEAK

At 13,065 feet, this peak is Nevada's second tallest and a defining feature of the park. Since park roads travel halfway up the mountain, it's not terribly difficult to hike up to its base and see its glacier.

ZION

UTAH • ESTABLISHED 1919 • 229 SQUARE MILES

I began my exploration of Utah's Mighty Five parks next, starting with Zion. A dramatic, awe-inspiring canyon is at the heart of the park, where sheer rock walls of red and tan Navajo sandstone plunge down to the Virgin River.

Zion sits at the intersection of the Colorado Plateau, the Great Basin, and the Mojave Desert. It's famous for having four distinct life zones to explore—low-elevation desert, riparian (or river banks), mid-elevation woodland, and high-elevation coniferous forest—that include mountains, plateaus, arches, monoliths, and more.

An incredible way to experience the park's grandeur is by hiking the steep Angel's Landing Trail. I hiked this 5.4-mile round-trip route, which took me to the top of a towering rock formation, revealing panoramic views of the canyon and the river far below. From this spot, I saw firsthand the glory of this place, where different ecosystems and formations collide.

3

4

1

❶ PRINCE'S PLUME
Stanleya pinnata
A perennial shrub with bright-yellow flowers that can grow up to five feet tall, this species thrives in arid and semi-desert conditions like those found in Zion.

❷ FREMONT'S COTTONWOOD
Populus fremontii
This tree grows near rivers and streams at lower elevations and can be found across the park, especially along the Virgin River. They can grow between 10 and 20 feet in a single year.

❸ BLACK-CHINNED HUMMINGBIRD
Archilochus alexandri
This species consumes nectar from flowers across the park and often makes its home in cottonwood trees.

❹ TIGER SALAMANDER
Ambystoma tigrinum
The largest land-dwelling salamander in the world, this species has a broad head and small eyes and is commonly seen at night after rainstorms.

❺ THE NARROWS
The narrowest part of Zion Canyon, where immense rock walls close in tightly on either side of the North Fork of the Virgin River, The Narrows present a unique opportunity to hike through shallow water deep into the canyon.

KID-FRIENDLY HIKE
The Watchman Trail
This moderately challenging 3.2-mile (round-trip) hike is best suited for older children and offers panoramic views of Zion Canyon and Watchman Peak.

BRYCE CANYON

UTAH • ESTABLISHED 1928 • 56 SQUARE MILES

Driving just under two hours east from Zion, I arrived at Bryce Canyon. From an overlook at Sunrise Point, I was immediately awestruck by my first views of the famous hoodoos that dominate this landscape.

Surprisingly, Bryce is not actually a canyon, but a group of natural amphitheaters carved into a high plateau, where the largest collection of hoodoos—irregular columns of orange and red rock formed by frost, weathering, and erosion—on Earth cover the terrain.

I hiked down from the overlook, surrounding myself with a world of rusty-orange rock, with every formation feeling so much grander the closer I got. Along the winding trail I saw impressive sights like Queen Victoria, The Gossips, Two Bridges, and Thor's Hammer.

Walking down here among so many towering rock spires carved by eons of time was so magical I didn't want to leave, and since there are so many trails that connect the amphitheaters, it's easy to spend all day exploring.

After hiking for a few hours, I took a rest before the Wall of Windows, where a few other folks were also sitting. I studied the intricate rock layers that had eroded over centuries to create the vista before me.

"If you think it's pretty now, you should come back in winter when the hoodoos are dusted with snow," a man with a baseball cap said loud enough so all of us could hear. "The white and orange together makes for quite a show."

❶ BLUE FLAX
Linum lewisii
The five petals of this wildflower range in color from white to deep blue. They can be found in the park along trails, in open fields, and near small shrubs.

❷ SCARLET GILIA
Ipomopsis aggregata
Also known as skyrocket, this plant is recognized by red, trumpet-shaped flowers that burst forth from a green stem. Hummingbirds often pollinate its blossoms, which also come in shades of white, orange, and pink.

❸ STELLER'S JAY
Cyanocitta stelleri
This bright-blue bird is loud and known to draw attention to itself with its distinct, sharp-voiced calls. It even imitates the sounds of other birds. Steller's jays feed on a variety of seeds, nuts, and insects.

❹ GREAT HORNED OWL
Bubo virginianus
These large, thick-bodied owls can be recognized by the two feathered tufts on their heads that resemble ears. They have the most diverse diet of all North American owls, consuming a variety of animals.

❺ THOR'S HAMMER
The most famous hoodoo in the park, this 150-foot-tall stone spire has a large block of sandstone on its top, making it resemble the hammer of the Norse god of thunder.

KID-FRIENDLY HIKE
Navajo Loop Trail
This 1.5-mile loop trail begins and ends at Sunset Point. It takes you down into the amphitheater of hoodoos and offers an up-close view of Thor's Hammer.

CAPITOL REEF

UTAH • ESTABLISHED 1971 • 378 SQUARE MILES

In the middle of southern Utah, an almost 100-mile long wrinkle disrupts the Earth's crust, creating a striking stretch of canyons, cliffs, and domes that you can't ignore, especially if you're trying to navigate around them. This is the Waterpocket Fold, a huge, 65-million-year-old feature that defines the park.

I saw the park's many layers of red-hued rocks by driving along the main park road and stopping to go for a few hikes.

I climbed up steep rock walls to reach the impressive Cassidy Arch, explored the sand-colored Capitol Gorge, and stood underneath the remarkable, nature-made Hickman Bridge, which rises up near the Fremont River.

❶

❷

❸

❶ SCARLET GLOBEMALLOW

Sphaeralcea coccinea

This bright-orange wildflower grows across the park among desert scrub, sagebrush, and ponderosa pine forests. Native communities commonly use it for medicinal purposes.

❷ RINGTAIL

Bassariscus astutus

Known for its bushy tail ringed with black and white, large eyes, and pointed snout, this member of the raccoon family is an excellent tree climber. It typically makes its den in small caves, hollow logs, or between large rocks near water.

❸ CATHEDRAL VALLEY

This area off the beaten path is full of huge sandstone monoliths that rise up like giants from the valley floor. It's well worth a visit, as standing before the Temple of the Sun and Temple of the Moon (the two most famous elevated rock formations here) is sure to take your breath away.

CANYONLANDS

UTAH • ESTABLISHED 1964 • 527 SQUARE MILES

I headed east and arrived at another red-and-orange rocky environment next, where canyons, mesas, and buttes abound.

Canyonlands is divided into four districts: Island in the Sky, the Needles, the Maze, and the Green and Colorado Rivers, which wind through the other three districts and have continuously carved stone away through the ages!

I decided to check out the Island in the Sky, the highest part of the park, made up of a broad, level mesa between the rivers. I was so high, I could see the other sections of the park far below! The vistas at the White Rim Overlook especially blew my mind, as I was in awe over how many canyons and spires could be seen from here.

❶ CLARET CUP CACTUS

Echinocereus triglochidiatus

A type of hedgehog cactus found across the Southwest, this species is spherical and tubular in nature, with the many prickly green parts of the cactus being overshadowed by the scarlet red cup-shaped flowers that bloom from its top.

❷ CANYON WREN

Catherpes mexicanus

This small bird can be hard to spot since its coloring blends in with its surroundings, but you may be able to hear its distinct, loud call echoing through the park's canyons.

❸ MESA ARCH

Prepare for epic views when you visit this formation, as this elongated natural stone arch stands on the edge of a cliff and perfectly frames the canyons and towers that populate the terrain below.

ARCHES

UTAH • ESTABLISHED 1971 • 120 SQUARE MILES

Not far from Canyonlands, there's a place that's famous for what time and the elements have created. Incredible arches have been carved by nature here, as the dry climate has shaped the brittle sandstone over the ages into jaw-dropping formations.

I explored my fifth and final park in Utah by visiting as many of these arches as I could. There are more than 2,000—the highest density in the world! Across this high desert, I walked along the Windows Loop and Turret Arch Trail, stood beneath the massive Double Arch, and gazed in wonder at the Landscape Arch, which is so long and thin it looks like it might collapse. The red-and-orange sandstone has been eroded into lofty pinnacles, huge fins, and enormous balanced rocks, too.

At the end of the day, while sitting before the famous Delicate Arch, I realized while looking at the eroded formations that something special had been created by what the natural elements wore away. "There can be beauty in what's missing," I said aloud, wanting my words to pair with the wind.

A small kangaroo rat scurried up beside me then, its gaze meeting mine as it paused, almost like it agreed with my thought.

My journey across America's national parks was approaching its final stretch, with most of my adventures behind me. Yet as I sat here and peered through the orange rock to gaze at the bright blue sky, dazzled by the complimentary colors found in nature, I knew my memories of this epic adventure would always be with me.

❶ UTAH JUNIPER

Juniperus osteosperma

This small conifer tree has needle-like leaves and produces blue-brown berries. Native Americans used different parts of the tree for a variety of medicinal purposes.

❷ BLACKBRUSH

Coleogyne ramosissima

This small shrub grows in shallow, sandy, and clay soils across the park. It is known for its dark grayish-green leaves and yellow flowers, which bloom in spring.

❸ ORD'S KANGAROO RAT

Dipodomys ordii

Known for eating plant matter and seeds, this golden-brown rat has a long tail with a bushy tip. It's uniquely adapted to living in the desert, as its body produces water by metabolizing the food it consumes.

❹ RED-TAILED HAWK

Buteo jamaicensis

Commonly seen flying across the sky in majestic flight patterns and making their distinctive screech call, this hawk species can be recognized by its red tail feathers.

❺ DELICATE ARCH

This 52-foot-tall freestanding natural arch is an icon of the park and the state of Utah. It towers over its surroundings, perched between a cliff and a deep panhole that plunges down dramatically.

KID-FRIENDLY HIKE

Double Arch Trail

This quick 0.6-mile (round-trip) hike takes you underneath the massive Double Arch and also offers views of other impressive arches in the area.

MESA VERDE

COLORADO • ESTABLISHED 1906 • 82 SQUARE MILES

In the southwestern corner of Colorado, this national park preserves the cultural heritage of the Ancestral Pueblo people and their incredible cliff dwellings, which are carved into the canyons found here.

With more than 600 cliff dwellings, Mesa Verde is the largest archaeological preserve in the United States, where you can witness the fascinating ways these buildings were constructed in the natural alcoves of the canyon walls.

Cliff Palace, the biggest of the cliff dwellings, is mostly made from sandstone, mortar, and wooden beams. It has more than 150 rooms and many of its buildings are multiple stories!

In addition to the history found here, the natural terrain of Mesa Verde is also incredible to explore, with canyons carved by rivers and streams, high mesas and plateaus overlooking the canyons, and many different plant communities including shrub-steppe and pinyon-juniper forests.

The Soda Canyon Overlook Trail was the perfect short hike to take at the end of the day, offering a 1.2-mile loop with views of the canyon and several cliff dwellings, including Balcony House.

"Isn't it nice to think people once lived in nature, building their homes right into these rocks?" a woman who was also enjoying the view asked me.

"It would be amazing if we still built our homes like this today," I answered. "Then maybe we'd all be as in touch with nature as we used to be."

❶ ROUND-LEAVED SNOWBERRY
Symphoricarpos rotundifolius
This shrub is part of the honeysuckle family and is known for its drooping, light-pink flowers and white berries, which usually grow together in pairs.

❷ GAMBEL OAK
Quercus gambelii
A drought-tolerant small tree that grows in the park's mountain shrub communities and woodlands, this species can regenerate even if it's damaged in a forest fire.

❸ NORTH AMERICAN PORCUPINE
Erethizon dorsatum
This species has a coat of about 30,000 quills (modified hairs formed into sharp, barbed, hollow spines) that are used for defense. A group of porcupines was once found at Cliff Palace, where they used the rock formations as a safe breeding spot.

❹ MEXICAN SPOTTED OWL
Strix occidentalis lucida
One of the largest owls in North America, with a nearly four-foot wingspan, this threatened species is an ashy-chestnut brown color and has white spots across its feathers. It prefers to nest in caves and alcoves along forested canyons.

❺ CLIFF CANYON
A deep, dramatic canyon of sandstone cliffs that was once a thriving neighborhood where the Ancestral Pueblo people lived and worked, this formation is best viewed from the various overlooks along its edges.

KID-FRIENDLY HIKE
Petroglyph Point Trail
This moderate 2.5-mile loop trail is best for older kids and offers amazing views of the Navajo and Spruce Canyons. It leads to a large, ancient petroglyph panel of humans, animals, and handprints etched into a rock wall.

❺

❹

❷

3

BLACK CANYON OF THE GUNNISON

COLORADO • ESTABLISHED 1999 • 47 SQUARE MILES

Quite unlike any other canyon in the country, this deep, steep, and narrow canyon has been carved by the Gunnison River and other natural forces for more than two million years. Standing at its edge can make you dizzy because of how dramatically it plunges, but even if you're afraid of heights, seeing it is well worth facing your fears.

Along the South Rim, I hiked the Warner Point Trail and the Oak Flat Loop Trail for beautiful views into the canyon. Its dark, sheer, grayish-black walls are etched deep into the Earth, separating the land between the Rocky Mountains and the Colorado Plateau.

The craggy rock spires along the canyon's edge and the huge scope of the Painted Wall were also incredible to see, showing off the uniqueness of this canyon, which is so narrow, you often can't see the river below.

❶ BIG SAGEBRUSH

Artemisia tridentata

An aromatic, pale gray-green shrub that grows in dry conditions, this plant provides food and habitat for many species, including the sage grouse and mule deer.

❷ BOBCAT

Lynx rufus

This stealthy wildcat mostly hunts rabbits and prefers living along canyons and plateaus. It gets its name from its black-tipped, "bobbed" tail.

❸ PAINTED WALL

At 2,250 feet, this is the tallest sheer cliff in Colorado. It's made of ancient gneiss and schist rocks that are crisscrossed with lines of lighter pegmatite rock, creating a striking canvas painted by nature.

GREAT SAND DUNES

COLORADO • ESTABLISHED 2004 • 233 SQUARE MILES

Here in south-central Colorado, the tallest sand dunes in North America pile toward the sky, reaching 750 feet high. I first spotted this massive 30-square-mile dune field from the camper, driving toward where the dunes lie along the edge of the Sangre de Cristo mountain range.

Once I arrived beside Medano Creek, I parked and hiked up the dunes, quickly making my way to the top of these huge sand piles.

There were gorgeous views of forests spreading back into the mountains in the distance as I got higher. It reminded me that this park has more than dunes to explore. Every step was a challenge because the sand shifted beneath my feet and the wind whipped grains at my face, but when I finally reached High Dune, I still wanted more!

❶ LEMON SCURFPEA
Psoralidium lanceolatum
The most common leafy plant you'll find growing on the dune field, this perennial bursts with tiny purple blossoms in spring, attracting insects to pollinate its flowers.

❷ AMERICAN BADGER
Taxidea taxus
Easily recognized by the black-and-white markings on its face, this species is found in the grasslands surrounding the dunes, hunting for rabbits and other small mammals.

❸ HIGH DUNE
Although this actually isn't the highest dune in the park, at 692 feet high, it's pretty close, and it's accessible from the main parking lot. From its top, you'll see epic views of the entire dune field and the adjacent mountains.

3

ROCKY MOUNTAIN

COLORADO • ESTABLISHED 1915 • 415 SQUARE MILES

❸

❺

In northern Colorado, where the Front Range of the Rocky Mountains rises high (as part of the Continental Divide), the last park of this great state waited for me. Driving in, I was amazed by the sheer size of these mountains.

This park is one of the highest in the nation, with 60 peaks over 12,000 feet high. Here you can explore alpine tundra, mountain forests, wide valleys that were carved by glaciers, and more than 350 miles of trails.

I hiked to Sky Pond on a heavenly route, stopping along the way to enjoy gorgeous Alberta Falls, before arriving at two adjacent alpine lakes, about five miles into the wilderness.

Lake of Glass came first, followed by Sky Pond, a turquoise-green lake that's nestled underneath a group of pointed, jagged peaks straight out of a storybook.

I sat near a park ranger with a wide-brimmed hat who was resting by the water's edge, and decided to eat the sandwich I'd packed for lunch. As I enjoyed the sights, I became distracted by a tiny American pika who began shrieking "Eep! Eep! Eep!" on a rock to my right, begging me to look.

"Why do you think he's squawking in such a peaceful place?" I asked the park ranger as we both stood up. I was feeling a bit cranky about the noise this small creature was making.

"This is its home," the ranger said softly. "It's most likely calling out to its family and friends." Immediately regretting my attitude, I reminded myself that although our national parks are open to all people, we're still just guests when we visit these protected lands.

❶ ROCKY MOUNTAIN COLUMBINE

Aquilegia coerulea

The state flower of Colorado, known for its lavender-blue petals, this species grows in both subalpine forests and rocky alpine sites.

❷ ELEPHANT'S HEAD

Pedicularis groenlandica

This showy wildflower gets its name from its magenta-colored blossoms, which resemble an elephant's head, complete with a trunk and droopy ears.

❸ WHITE-TAILED PTARMIGAN

Lagopus leucura

Known to inhabit alpine areas of the park, this member of the grouse family is brown and gray during the summer and bright white in the winter. Its tail remains white all year.

❹ AMERICAN PIKA

Ochotona princeps

This small rabbit relative has distinct round ears and is gray to cinnamon-brown in color. It typically lives in boulder fields or above the tree line, snacking on a variety of plants. Very vocal, it calls out to warn of predators and to attract other pikas during breeding season.

❺ SKY POND

One of the park's most famous alpine lakes, Sky Pond has super clear water that's drained by Icy Brook. Towering above the lake are the Cathedral Spires, a group of unforgettable peaks that will make you feel tiny.

KID-FRIENDLY HIKE

Bear Lake Loop

A flat, easy 0.7-mile loop trail that circles Bear Lake and offers lovely views of the surrounding mountains, this hike is perfect for families with young children.

WIND CAVE

SOUTH DAKOTA • ESTABLISHED 1903 • 53 SQUARE MILES

I drove five hours north to the Black Hills, heading underground on a tour led by a park ranger to see Wind Cave's famous boxwork formations. These thin calcite blades crisscross in honeycomb patterns on the ceilings and walls, forming hundreds of "boxes."

I learned that it's a "breathing cave," because there's different air pressure between the inside and outside. The air flows back and forth like the wind, which is how the cave was named.

After my tour, I explored aboveground, hiking on the Centennial Trail, which cut through prairies and ponderosa forests. Along the way, I spotted black-footed ferrets popping out from the grass time and again, as if they were playing a game.

❶ PRAIRIE BLUEBELL

Mertensia lanceolata

This plant has eye-catching flowers that change from a pinkish-purple to blue as they open, with multiple buds hanging down from its stalk in trumpet-like shapes.

❷ BLACK-FOOTED FERRET

Mustela nigripes

Brought back from the edge of extinction, this species has a long slender body with light fur and a dark "bandit mask." About 90 percent of its diet comes from consuming prairie dogs, which it lives alongside in burrows, coming out to hunt them at night.

❸ WIND CAVE

The first cave to become a national park worldwide, Wind Cave is the densest cave system ever discovered, with the greatest passage volume per cubic mile. Renowned for its calcite formations, it claims 95 percent of the world's discovered boxwork.

BADLANDS

SOUTH DAKOTA • ESTABLISHED 1978 • 379 SQUARE MILES

My next park was just two hours east, where a rugged landscape of colorful eroded buttes, spires, and pinnacles dominate the terrain. These fascinating badlands look like tan, orange, and rust colored sandcastles, which have been created by rocks gradually building up (deposition), and then gradually wearing down (erosion).

I began in the park's north unit, where dozens of impressive overlooks along the park road allowed me to look out at multicolored badlands. I took my time at each stop to study their intricate layers.

The park has one of the world's richest fossil beds, where remains of ancient horses and rhinos have been found. It's also home to the largest undisturbed mixed grass prairie in the country.

1

2

3

❶ BLUE GRAMA

Bouteloua gracilis

This long-living grass is actually green or gray. It's low-growing and drought tolerant, with comb-like spikes that push out from its flowering stem.

❷ BLACK-TAILED PRAIRIE DOG

Cynomys ludovicianus

This species has strong, short arms with long-nailed toes, which are perfect for digging burrows underground, where they live and hide from predators. Highly social animals, they live in colonies like the one at Roberts Prairie Dog Town, where you can see them up close and hear their high-pitched squeaks.

❸ BADLANDS WALL

This wall, which runs from east to west, is made up of the park's famous rock formations, formed by erosion. It separates the lower prairie to the south and the upper prairie to the north.

THEODORE ROOSEVELT

NORTH DAKOTA • ESTABLISHED 1978 • 110 SQUARE MILES

This is the only national park to be named after a person (who happened to be our 26th president). The land found here in western North Dakota is home to colorful badlands, grassy prairies, a petrified forest, and a wide variety of wildlife.

The park is divided into sections—a north unit, south unit, and Roosevelt's Elkhorn Ranch—and the Little Missouri River winds through all three, connecting the separate parts of the park.

The south unit is the most visited, because it's the easiest to get to. This is where I spent my time, driving in the camper and peering out at the badlands, their layers of multihued rocks on full display as I cruised by. I stopped at many of the overlooks along the park road (which you can take as one long scenic loop drive), often spotting bison and wild horses roaming freely in the distance.

❶ PRAIRIE CONEFLOWER

Ratibida columnifera

This perennial wildflower is resistant to drought and shows off pretty blossoms in midsummer across the park's prairies, providing nectar and pollen for bees and butterflies.

❷ PRAIRIE ROSE

Rosa arkansana

The state flower of North Dakota, this species can be found across the park's grasslands, bursting with bright-pink blossoms in late May and early June.

❸ WILD HORSE

Equus ferus

Descendants of domesticated horses that were originally brought here by European settlers, these wild horses are typically seen in groups of 5 to 15. While they range in color and size, each group has a dominant male stallion who leads the mares and their offspring.

❹ WILD TURKEY

Meleagris gallopavo

A notable year-round resident of the park, this large bird roosts in the forested areas and forages in the wide-open prairies.

❺ LITTLE MISSOURI RIVER

A tributary of the Missouri River, this body of water flows northward through all three units of the park. A great place to see it is along the Wind Canyon Trail, which takes you along an elevated bluff above where the river flows.

KID-FRIENDLY HIKE

Boicourt Overlook Trail

This easy 0.8-mile (round-trip) trail is located halfway along the South Unit scenic drive, which makes it a great place to stop and explore with superb views of the badlands.

VOYAGEURS

MINNESOTA • ESTABLISHED 1975 • 341 SQUARE MILES

The land of 10,000 lakes was my next stopping point, as I drove to the waters of Minnesota's northern border. Voyageurs, named after the French-Canadian fur traders who once paddled here, is 40 percent water with over 30 lakes, including Rainy, Kabetogama, Namakan, and Sand Point, which are the largest, in that order.

I decided to go on the guided Grand Tour of Rainy Lake with a park ranger, since the best way to explore here is by boat. Cruising around the lake, I came to better understand how this park is a mixture of water, forests, islands, and rocks. From where I sat comfortably, afloat, I also spotted a number of black-and-white birds with startling red eyes as we sped along.

While peering out at bright-blue water studded with small rocky islands covered in thick green pines, I remembered that my adventure across America's national parks would soon come to an end and I felt a bit down. "Why so sad, young fellow?" A woman asked as she took a seat next to me.

"Pretty soon I'll be done exploring every national park in the United States," I said, sighing. "It's been such an amazing adventure, a part of me wishes it could go on forever."

❶ JACK PINE

Pinus banksiana

Typically found along the shores of the park's many lakes, this pine species does not grow perfectly straight, often resulting in an irregular shape.

❷ INKY CAP

Coprinopsis atramentaria

This gray-brown fungus has a cap that's tinged with black. It's commonly found on the Echo Bay Trail, growing in large clumps alongside tree trunks and stumps. While its black ink was once used for printing, it's poisonous, so don't pick it or eat it!

❸ COMMON LOON

Gavia immer

The state bird of Minnesota, this water-loving, diving bird is known for its eerie yodel-like calls. Its large black body is checkered with a distinct white pattern, making it easily recognizable, while its red eyes help it see underwater.

❹ COMMON SNAPPING TURTLE

Chelydra serpentina

The largest turtle found in the park, this species can weigh up to 35 pounds. They eat everything from fish, frogs, birds, and snakes to small mammals. Look for them near the water's edge, sunning themselves on rocks.

❺ RAINY LAKE

Straddling the border between Minnesota and Canada, this enormous freshwater lake covers 360 square miles. The remnant of a larger, ancient lake that was once carved by glaciers, it has a jagged, rocky shoreline and more than 2,200 islands dotting its waters.

KID-FRIENDLY HIKE

Blind Ash Bay Trail

This moderate 3.0-mile lollipop trail leads you deep into the boreal forest and ends at a stunning overlook with views of Kabetogama Lake.

ISLE ROYALE

MICHIGAN • ESTABLISHED 1940 • 893 SQUARE MILES

An isolated island environment of pure wilderness found in the northwest corner of Lake Superior, this national park is untouched by time.

I arrived on a boat at Windigo Harbor and hiked away from the rocky shore. I headed into the woods on the Feldtmann Lake Trail, passing through a boreal forest of balsam fir, spruce pines, and wild berries to snack on. The hike was peaceful and quiet, perhaps because there's only a third of the mainland mammal species present here, with wolves and moose being the most famous.

I camped overnight, then took a boat to the island's other side, exploring Rock Harbor and hiking down to Scoville Point.

❶ PINK LADY'S SLIPPER

Cypripedium acaule

This orchid's pink, showy flowers grow in a pouch-like shape that resemble a lady's slipper. It grows in damp woods, bogs, and open areas that offer sunlight and shade.

❷ GRAY WOLF

Canis lupus

The main predator here since its arrival across an ice bridge from Canada in the 1940s, this mammal has a thick, gray fur coat and grows up to six feet long. It typically hunts for smaller prey, but will go after moose when hunting in a pack.

❸ SCOVILLE POINT

A picturesque end of a rocky peninsula with spectacular views of smaller nearby islands, this is the place to go if you want to capture Isle Royale's mix of clear-blue water, tall green trees, and rocky shores in one perfect shot.

INDIANA DUNES

INDIANA • ESTABLISHED 2019 • 24 SQUARE MILES

Back on the mainland, I drove to the southern shore of Lake Michigan, where this park stretches on for 15 miles, with lots of its land covered by sand. The sand dunes here have been formed by glaciers, water, and wind over the past 14,000 years, with some piling to heights of 200 feet.

I walked along the sandy shores of Lake Michigan, then hiked up the dunes, getting an elevated view of the massive lake, which stretches to the horizon. The trail I found led me away from the dunes and into different habitats; I came across bogs, marshes, prairies, and forests. I saw tons of plant species and fascinating birds, which makes sense, as this small but mighty park is very biologically diverse!

❶ SIX-LINED RACERUNNER
Aspidoscelis sexlineatus
Often found scuttling along the sand dunes, this small lizard gets its name from the six yellow stripes that run down its body from head to tail.

❷ PURPLE PITCHER PLANT
Sarracenia purpurea
This carnivorous plant can be found in Pinhook Bog, where it traps insects in its pitcher-shaped leaves. The small hairs on its petals prevent insects from escaping once captured.

❸ LAKE MICHIGAN
The second-largest of the Great Lakes in terms of depth and overall volume, Lake Michigan is the only Great Lake fully located within the US, with the states of Wisconsin, Illinois, Indiana, and Michigan bordering it.

3

GATEWAY ARCH

MISSOURI • ESTABLISHED 2018 • 0.14 SQUARE MILES

Along the mighty Mississippi, our smallest national park by far sits in Missouri, originally constructed to recognize the westward expansion of our country.

This is our only national park where the main feature is a monument, and if it were up to me, it'd be a national monument instead—but because Congress designated it a national park, I had to visit it. The monument is the Gateway Arch, a 630-foot-tall steel arch that dominates the park and the St. Louis skyline.

I took the elevator-like tram that's hidden inside the arch to the observation room at its top and was rewarded with cool views of the city and beyond. Back on the ground afterward, I strolled around the tiny park, walking through the grassy fields and past the human-made ponds.

1 BIG BLUESTEM
Andropogon gerardii
Found in the native grass meadow section of the park, this tall grass typically grows in bunches across the Great Plains and central prairies.

2 EASTERN GRAY SQUIRREL
Sciurus carolinensis
This squirrel is one of the most common animals to be found here, where it can be seen climbing trees as it searches for berries, seeds, acorns, and nuts to eat.

3 MISSISSIPPI RIVER
The primary river of the United States, with the largest drainage basin, the Mississippi divides the country between east and west. It starts in Minnesota and runs south for 2,340 miles, passing through nine other states before reaching the Gulf of Mexico.

MAMMOTH CAVE

KENTUCKY • ESTABLISHED 1941 • 83 SQUARE MILES

My penultimate (second-to-last) park took me underground again, as I explored the world's longest cave system, which is hidden beneath Kentucky's rolling hills. I joined the ranger-led Grand Avenue Tour, which took me through four miles of underground slot canyons, tubular passageways, and tunnels sparkling with gypsum—all kinds of thrills!

Walking along the cave's passageways for so long made me realize just how huge it is. With 412 miles of surveyed routes that stay at 54°F year-round, you could spend a lifetime exploring.

Back above ground, I strolled the Green River Bluff Trail, which led me along a forested ridge that offered lovely views of the river meandering below.

❶ TRUE PASSIONFLOWER
Passiflora incarnata
Growing in long vines that can extend for over 25 feet, this species is also known as the maypop and is famous for its intricate bluish-purple flowers and fleshy fruit.

❷ KENTUCKY CAVE SHRIMP
Palaemonias ganteri
This endangered crustacean is only found in the base-level cave streams that flow here. They spend their entire lives in these caves and have no eyes, instead using antennae to find their food. Their colorless shells make them transparent and hard to spot.

❸ THE ROTUNDA
A large, circular underground room that's a quarter-acre in size and 140 feet below the surface, this frequently visited room was created by rivers that once flowed through here, carving away at the limestone rock and forming a natural breakout dome.

CUYAHOGA VALLEY

OHIO • ESTABLISHED 2000 • 51 SQUARE MILES

In between Cleveland and Akron in Northeast Ohio, this wildlife haven is home to dense forests, deep gorges, and rocky waterfalls. When I arrived, I almost couldn't believe it—this was my final national park!

At the visitor center, I learned about how the Ohio and Erie Canal was built here and how the Cuyahoga River used to be so polluted it caught on fire multiple times! Luckily, the area's designation as a national park has led to it being conserved and cleaned up.

Heading back outdoors, I decided to go deep into the woods to get away from the roads that crisscross the park by hiking on the Buckeye Trail for a few miles. Eventually, I arrived at Blue Hen Falls, a peaceful little waterfall that cuts across layers of rock.

Next, I visited Brandywine Falls, Cuyahoga's iconic cascade, which flows through a rocky gorge that you can access along an elevated boardwalk.

Standing before the falls, I closed my eyes, wanting to focus on the sound of the water falling. When I opened them a minute later, dozens of monarch butterflies swirled around me, their orange-and-black wings flapping against the breeze.

One of them landed on my shoulder and as it did I decided to whisper aloud: "I may have visited every national park in America now, but there's still so much more nature to see." The butterfly flew away with its delicate wings to join the others. As I watched them float past the waterfall and head into the woods, I couldn't help but wonder... What's next?

❶ ❸

❶ AMERICAN SYCAMORE

Platanus occidentalis

This large deciduous tree often reaches between 75 and 100 feet tall and grows along streambanks and bottomlands. The oldest one found here is referred to as the Moses Cleaveland Tree, and it's nearly 400 years old.

❷ YELLOW TROUT LILY

Erythronium americanum

This golden-hued wildflower grows in the woods along steep slopes and stream banks. The brown pattern on its gray-green leaves resembles the coloring of a brook trout, for which it gets its name.

❸ GREAT BLUE HERON

Ardea herodias

The largest heron in North America, this elegant bird's numbers have soared here since the ecosystem was first protected and efforts were made to start cleaning up the river in 1974. It nests in the park's wetlands and explores along the river's path.

❹ MONARCH BUTTERFLY

Danaus plexippus

Known to stop in Cuyahoga Valley to lay their eggs on milkweed plants and rest during their 2,000-mile annual migration from Mexico to Canada, this species is the most widely recognized butterfly in North America.

❺ BRANDYWINE FALLS

With a height of 60 feet, this cascade has been carving the sandstone and shale rock layers around it for over 10,000 years, since the last glacial retreat.

KID-FRIENDLY HIKE

Ledges Trail

This 2.4-mile loop trail showcases impressive rock formations, narrow passageways, a natural cave, and an overlook with a panoramic view of the valley.

2
5
4

After months on the road, my adventures around America came to an end. I returned home to Western Pennsylvania and parked the camper in my driveway. Before heading inside, I thought about all I'd seen. A highlight reel of magical, natural wonders scrolled through my mind.

I'd been lucky enough to visit every national park in the United States, and I was in total awe of how the glorious power of nature had created so much beauty. From glacier-capped mountains to cacti-covered deserts, from red-rock canyons to moss-drenched rainforests—I realized that our planet is such a special place, where millions of different species live across a variety of environments.

While Mother Earth does a fantastic job guiding them through life the best she can, there's so much more we can do as human beings to help protect our natural surroundings and strive for a better balance that serves all creatures.

If I could urge you to do one thing, it would be to go outside and immerse yourself in nature. It doesn't even have to be a national park (though of course, those are great)—heading into the woods behind your backyard or to a city park works just as well. Take notice of all the interesting plants and animals you see, and try to figure out what is unique about them.

As my mind raced with all of these thoughts, and I dreamed of visiting even more national parks in other countries, I followed my own advice and turned toward the nearby creek. I ambled down the old path I've known since I was a boy and walked along the water, listening to the robins sing in the trees.

The joy of being in nature brought me a sense of peace and happiness with every step I took. I knew I would never again take time spent outside for granted. I told myself that I would continue to spend time immersed in nature throughout all the days of my life, while striving to help preserve it and educate others about all the magic it holds.

I hope you'll do the same.

FACTS

MOST VISITED (2024 YEARLY NUMBERS)

1. **GREAT SMOKY MOUNTAINS** – 12,191,834 visitors
2. **ZION** – 4,946,592 visitors
3. **GRAND CANYON** – 4,919,163 visitors
4. **YELLOWSTONE** – 4,744,353 visitors
5. **ROCKY MOUNTAIN** – 4,154,349 visitors
6. **YOSEMITE** – 4,121,807 visitors
7. **ACADIA** – 3,961,661 visitors
8. **OLYMPIC** – 3,717,267 visitors
9. **GRAND TETON** – 3,628,222 visitors
10. **GLACIER** – 3,208,755 visitors

OLDEST PARKS

1. **YELLOWSTONE** – 1872
2. **SEQUOIA** – 1890
3. **YOSEMITE** – 1890
4. **MOUNT RAINIER** – 1899
5. **CRATER LAKE** – 1902
6. **WIND CAVE** – 1903
7. **MESA VERDE** – 1906
8. **GLACIER** – 1910
9. **ROCKY MOUNTAIN** – 1915
10. **HAWAII VOLCANOES** – 1916

LEAST VISITED (2024 YEARLY NUMBERS)

1. **GATES OF THE ARCTIC** – 11,907 visitors
2. **NORTH CASCADES** – 16,485 visitors
3. **KOBUK VALLEY** – 17,233 visitors
4. **LAKE CLARK** – 18,505 visitors
5. **AMERICAN SAMOA** – 22,567 visitors
6. **ISLE ROYALE** – 28,806 visitors
7. **KATMAI** – 36,230 visitors
8. **WRANGELL-ST. ELIAS** – 81,670 visitors
9. **DRY TORTUGAS** – 84,873 visitors
10. **GREAT BASIN** – 152,068 visitors

NEWEST PARKS

1. **NEW RIVER GORGE** – 2020
2. **WHITE SANDS** – 2019
3. **INDIANA DUNES** – 2019
4. **GATEWAY ARCH** – 2018
5. **PINNACLES** – 2013
6. **GREAT SAND DUNES** – 2004
7. **CONGAREE** – 2003
8. **CUYAHOGA VALLEY** – 2000
9. **BLACK CANYON OF THE GUNNISON** – 1999
10. **DEATH VALLEY & JOSHUA TREE** – 1994

BIGGEST

1. **WRANGELL-ST. ELIAS** - 20,587 square miles
2. **GATES OF THE ARCTIC** - 13,238 square miles
3. **DENALI** - 9,492 square miles
4. **KATMAI** - 6,395 square miles
5. **LAKE CLARK** - 6,297 square miles
6. **DEATH VALLEY** - 5,347 square miles
7. **GLACIER BAY** - 5,125 square miles
8. **YELLOWSTONE** - 3,472 square miles
9. **KOBUK VALLEY** - 2,736 square miles
10. **EVERGLADES** - 2,358 square miles

SMALLEST

1. **GATEWAY ARCH** - 0.14 square miles
2. **HOT SPRINGS** - 9 square miles
3. **AMERICAN SAMOA** - 21 square miles
4. **VIRGIN ISLANDS** - 23 square miles
5. **INDIANA DUNES** - 24 square miles
6. **PINNACLES** - 42 square miles
7. **CONGAREE** - 42 square miles
8. **BLACK CANYON OF THE GUNNISON** - 47 square miles
9. **CUYAHOGA VALLEY** - 51 square miles
10. **HALEAKALĀ** - 52 square miles

STATES WITH THE MOST PARKS

1. **CALIFORNIA** - 9
2. **ALASKA** - 8
3. **UTAH** - 5
4. **COLORADO** - 4
5. **WASHINGTON/FLORIDA/ARIZONA** - 3

PARKS WITH PRESERVES*

DENALI
GATES OF THE ARCTIC
GLACIER BAY
GREAT SAND DUNES
KATMAI
LAKE CLARK
NEW RIVER GORGE
WRANGELL-ST. ELIAS

AUTHOR'S NOTE

When this book was completed in November 2025, the United States had 63 national parks—all of which are included here. One of the great things about the National Park Service is that new parks can be added, so there may be additional national parks by the time you read this. While we couldn't predict the future to include them, we hope these new parks will protect more important flora, fauna, and formations for generations to come.

All of the real photographs in this book were taken by me during my travels to every national park in the United States from 2015 to 2025.

Each national park has a detailed web page created by the National Park Service that includes important updates and information. To learn more about the parks or to find a specific park page, visit www.nps.gov.

*Square miles noted for these parks includes both areas.

MULTI-PARK TRIPS

IF YOU'RE LOOKING TO EXPLORE A FEW PARKS AT A TIME, BUT NOT ALL 63 IN ONE TRIP, THESE OPTIONS ARE GREAT GROUPINGS TO CONSIDER!

ALASKA INTRO ❑

DENALI
KENAI FJORDS
WRANGELL-ST. ELIAS

APPALACHIA ❑

GREAT SMOKY MOUNTAINS
NEW RIVER GORGE
SHENANDOAH

CALIFORNIA CLASSIC ❑

KINGS CANYON
LASSEN VOLCANIC
REDWOOD
SEQUOIA
YOSEMITE

COLORADO CIRCUIT ❑

BLACK CANYON OF THE GUNNISON
GREAT SAND DUNES
MESA VERDE
ROCKY MOUNTAIN

CONTINENTAL DIVIDE ❑

GLACIER
GRAND TETON
YELLOWSTONE

* CHECK THE BOXES ❑ OF THE PARKS YOU HAVE VISITED.

DESERT VIBES ❑

DEATH VALLEY
GRAND CANYON
JOSHUA TREE
SAGUARO

GREAT LAKES ❑

INDIANA DUNES
ISLE ROYALE
VOYAGEURS

PACIFIC ISLANDS ❑

AMERICAN SAMOA
HALEAKALĀ
HAWAII VOLCANOES

PACIFIC NORTHWEST ❑

CRATER LAKE
MOUNT RAINIER
NORTH CASCADES
OLYMPIC

SOUTHWEST WONDERS ❑

BIG BEND
CARLSBAD CAVERNS
GUADALUPE MOUNTAINS
WHITE SANDS

UTAH MIGHTY FIVE ❑

ARCHES
BRYCE CANYON
CANYONLANDS
CAPITOL REEF
ZION

WET & WILD FLORIDA ❑

BISCAYNE
DRY TORTUGAS
EVERGLADES

GLOSSARY

ALPINE an environment found in mountainous areas where the elevation is too high for trees to grow, but low enough to be below the permanent snowline.

ANCIENT having existed for many years, typically before most human civilizations.

BADLANDS areas of land that are heavily eroded into geologic formations, with little vegetation.

BOREAL a habitat found in far northern regions that are dominated by coniferous forests.

BUTTE a single hill or mountain with steep sides and a flat top, smaller than a mesa.

CALDERA a large volcanic crater formed by a major eruption that led to the collapse of the volcano's mouth.

CANYON a deep, narrow valley or gorge with steep sides, it usually has a stream or river flowing through it.

CASCADE another name for a waterfall, typically one that falls in stages down a rocky slope or cliff.

CAVE a natural chamber or series of chambers found underground, often in the side of a hill or cliff.

CLIFF a steep, vertical rock face that plummets dramatically to the land or water below it, often found at the edge of the sea.

CLIMATE the weather conditions that regularly occur in an area over a long period of time.

COAST the edge of land that meets the ocean, often sandy or rocky.

CONIFEROUS evergreen trees that keep their needle-like leaves year-round.

CONTINENTAL DIVIDE a series of mountain ranges that divides the land and separates watersheds, which flow into different oceans from there.

CRATER a bowl-shaped indentation in the Earth, often around the mouth of a volcano.

DECIDUOUS trees that lose their leaves every autumn and regrow them in the spring.

DIVERSE displaying a great deal of variety and differences, especially when comparing species.

ECOSYSTEM a biological community of organisms that interact with one another in the same physical environment.

ELEVATION the height to which something reaches, typically above sea level.

ENVIRONMENT the conditions of the natural world as a whole in a given area that affect the species who live there.

EROSION the gradual process of being worn away by natural forces like water, wind, and ice.

EVERGREEN another name for a coniferous tree that keeps its leaves throughout the year.

EXTINCT when a species no longer has any living members anywhere on Earth.

FAUNA the animal life found in a particular region or habitat.

FLORA the plant life found in a particular region or habitat.

FOREST a large area that is densely covered with trees and undergrowth.

FORMATION a natural geological feature or landform with distinct physical characteristics that set it apart from its surroundings.

FOSSIL the preserved remnants or remains of ancient plant or animal species that have been protected in the Earth's crust.

GEYSER a spring that functions like a natural water fountain, shooting hot water and steam high into the air.

GLACIER a slow-moving, long-lasting, huge collection of compacted ice that forms on land and spreads downward to lower elevations due to gravity.

GROVE a group of trees clustered together with little or no undergrowth present.

HABITAT the place or environment where a species is naturally well-suited to live its life.

HIKE a long walk through nature that follows a trail and usually climbs upward.

HOODOO a naturally formed column of rock or pinnacle that's created by weathering and erosion.

HOT SPRING a place where naturally hot water that is heated by volcanic activity far underground emerges from the Earth's surface.

ISLAND an area of land that is surrounded by water and separate from other landforms.

LAKE a considerable body of standing water found inland and surrounded by land.

LANDSCAPE all of the visible features or natural scenery of an area of land or wilderness that can be considered together as a whole.

LAVA hot molten or semifluid rock that has erupted from a volcano or fissure in the Earth's crust.

LOWER 48 also called the contiguous 48, this refers to the connected 48 states in central North America, excluding Alaska and Hawaii.

MAINLAND a large, continuous piece of land that includes the greater part of a country as opposed to offshore islands or other separate territories.

MANGROVE tropical trees or shrubs that grow mainly in coastal saline or brackish water in large groups, often helping prevent coastal erosion.

MARSH an area of low-lying land that is often flooded and remains waterlogged, typically covered in tall grasses and cattails.

MESA an isolated flat-topped area with steep sides that is naturally elevated from its surroundings; larger than a butte but smaller than a plateau.

MONOLITH a large single upright stone formation that is in the shape of a column or pillar.

MOUNTAIN a large natural elevation of the Earth's surface that rises dramatically from the surrounding terrain.

NATURE the physical world that surrounds us that is not human-made, including plants, animals, landscapes, and other natural features.

OVERLOOK a place where you can look down or out from to enjoy an inspiring view of the surrounding landscape.

PARK RANGER a park employee who is responsible for protecting and managing the natural and cultural resources within their designated park.

PEAK the highest elevated point at the top of a mountain.

PENINSULA a portion of land that is surrounded by water on three sides and connected to a larger piece of land.

PERENNIAL a plant or flower that lives for more than two years with recurring growth and blooms.

PETRIFIED organic matter that has changed into a stony substance through a slow process called mineralization.

PINNACLE a high, pointed piece of rock that stretches toward the sky.

PLATEAU an extensive and flat piece of land that is elevated sharply above its surrounding terrain.

PRAIRIE a large tract of mostly flat grassland that is typically treeless.

RAINFOREST a temperate or tropical woodland with rich biodiversity, dense vegetation, and consistent, heavy amounts of rainfall.

RANGE a series of mountains that are generally clustered together in a row and connected by high ground.

REGION a broad area that's distinguished by similar geographic features and species.

REMOTE a place that is situated far away from the main centers of population.

ROUTE an established way of travel from one point to another.

SANDSTONE a warm-colored sedimentary rock that is easily eroded, it consists of quartz grains cemented together.

SEA the large expanse of oceanic salt water that covers most of Earth's surface and surrounds its land masses.

SHORE the land bordering a large body of water, such as a lake or the sea.

SPECIES a class of organisms that has the same characteristics and is capable of breeding and producing fertile offspring.

SPIRE the tall protruding part of a formation that typically tapers toward its top.

TEMPERATE a moderate climate with mild temperatures and high amounts of rainfall.

TERRAIN a stretch of land or geographic area that usually shares similar physical features.

TREK a challenging hike or long walk that follows a trail and immerses you into nature.

TROPICAL a region or climate that is frost-free, with high temperatures that support year-round plant growth.

TUNDRA a vast, treeless terrain type found in the Arctic and subarctic where the ground is permanently frozen.

UNDERGROUND beneath the surface of the Earth, where cave systems are found.

VALLEY an extended low area of land between hills or mountains that often has a river or stream running through it.

VARIETY the quality or state of being different or diverse, especially when comparing biodiversity in an ecosystem.

VEGETATION the plant life considered collectively across a particular area or habitat.

VISTA a fabulous view that can be seen at a particular location, especially from an elevated spot or at a narrow opening.

VOLCANO a mountain or hill that has a vent that reaches down into the Earth's crust from which steam and molten rock can be pushed through, sometimes known to erupt violently.

WATERFALL a cascade of falling water that typically flows off a cliff or other elevated precipice onto lower ground below.

WETLAND areas of land such as marshes or swamps that are often covered in shallow water, saturating the soil.

WILDERNESS an untamed and untouched area of land where no humans permanently reside, allowing the flora and fauna who live there to thrive.

ALEXANDER M. RIGBY
—AUTHOR—

Alexander M. Rigby has visited every national park in the United States. He is an avid traveler and has been fortunate enough to explore stunning natural landscapes across six continents. Alexander is a *New York Times* bestselling editor at Penguin Random House, where he has overseen titles such as *Baking Across America* and *Life on Svalbard*. He holds an MFA from Stonecoast at the University of Southern Maine. Alexander lives in Pittsburgh, Pennsylvania, with his husband and their Portuguese water dog, Cooper Atticus. Learn more at arigby.com.

QU LAN
–ILLUSTRATOR–

QU Lan was born and raised in China. After studying oil painting at the China Academy of Art, she moved to France, where she first worked as a designer before turning fully to illustration. Since her first book was published in 2010, she has built a solid career as a children's book illustrator, with numerous titles released in the United States, France, the United Kingdom, and China. *The Nature of Our National Parks* is the second book Qu Lan has illustrated for Tra Publishing. The first, *Supernavigators, How Animals Find Their Way* was published in 2025.